My Personal War Within

My Personal War Within

"A Struggle to Find Inner Peace"

Ted Bagley

Copyright © 2020 by Ted Bagley.

ISBN-978-1-6455-0857-1

All rights reserved. No part of this book may be reproduced or transmitted in any form or by any means, electronic or mechanical, including photocopying, recording, or by any information storage and retrieval system, without permission in writing from the copyright owner.

The views expressed in this work are solely those of the author and do not necessarily reflect the views of the publisher, and the publisher hereby disclaims any responsibility for them.

Matchstick Literary
1-888-306-8885
orders@matchliterary.com

Contents

Acknowledgement 9

Preface 13

Introduction 17

Chapter I   Planning the trip 19

Chapter II   The Beginning 45

Chapter III   Bare Necessities 52

Chapter IV   The Early Years 58

Chapter V   Character Builders 66

Chapter VI   The Middle Years 72

Chapter VII   Later Years 78

Chapter VIII   Considering the Army 83

Chapter IX   Life in the Army 91

Chapter X   The External War 101

Chapter XI   Home Coming 113

Chapter XII   Entering Corporate America 118

Chapter XIII   My Person Beliefs 139

Chapter XIV   Infectious quotes 151

Conclusion 169

Recommended Reading 179

This book is dedicated to the memory of my parents Ted and Eddie Mae Bagley, who passed away in 1996 and 1998 respectively. Also I would like to honor the memory of my sister Mrs. Elizabeth "Bonny" Fitts, who passed in 2007 and her beloved husband Carl "Mop" Fitts, who passed in March, 2008, unexpectedly and just eight months after his beloved wife Liz. These memories would not have been complete without them. The love and wisdom given to my brother Bill and me by them, over the years, will continue to give direction to our lives.

Their footsteps are forever present with us. Our lives were made richer because of their being a part of it and we are eternally grateful that God shared them with us for a given period.

Acknowledgement

The ultimate measure of a person is not where he or she stands in moments of comfort and convenience, but where he or she stands in moments of challenge and adversity.
—Dr. Martin Luther King, Jr.

As I have pieced these personal and hopefully interesting facts together over the past few years, there were those who made significant contributions in bringing this work to completion. It's important that I acknowledge their input to my personal war within."

Though she is no longer with me, I want to thank my mother for supplying many of the facts found in this book. She truly loved me unconditionally, no matter how much of a pest I was in accumulating these artifacts and sound bites of the past. I have never been called so many names, both good and bad, as there were during the precious last years that I was blessed to have shared with her. Though she was a very spiritual and God-filled lady, her tongue was as sharp as her recitation of Bible verses. She passed on to her heavenly home during the year 1998.

I would also like to honor my father, who passed on to glory in 1996, for providing the role model and strict discipline that was needed not only to fight my war within, but also to understand how it personally affected me and the person that I am today. He was a man of few words but those words were usually tough and straight to the point. My dad was not a warm and visibly caring individual but I knew he had an invisible soft spot based on his actions and undeniable love for his family. The true soul of a man is rooted not only in what he says but what he does.

A special thanks goes to my sister Liz, for her excellent verbal and editing skills as well as that tart tongue which she inherited from my mother. My sister always had that encouraging attitude that motivated me to finish what I start. I guess that was the professor in her. Since it has taken me a few years to complete this book, Liz was diagnosed with lung cancer from the many years of smoking **two** packs of cigarettes a day. Unfortunately, though a tremendous fighter she had proven to be, she lost her battle to this terrible disease in July of 2007. A special and heart felt thanks goes to my final editor and friend Shante Morgan Durisseau for laboring diligently on the project.

A cautious but heartfelt thanks goes to my brother Bill for threatening legal action if I strayed from what he considers the "true facts." He and I have been very close over the years. His wisdom and candor has a way of cutting to the chase on issues and if I'm not prepared for a straight and candid answer, then I don't ask the question. If I needed a shoulder, Bill was always there. The advantage I have always had over both Bill and Liz is that I still remember details and they didn't remember who they were half the time.

And what can I say about my brother-in-law, Carl I. "Mop" Fitts. He was one of a kind and he will be truly missed. He was small in stature but had a heart as big as life itself. Carl was more like a brother to both Bill and me than a brother-in-law. There was nothing that we could ask within reason that Carl would not try to provide. Their home was the family meeting place once our parents were deceased: 1555 Merriweather Circle, Montgomery, Ala. will be forever etched into my memory bank and the bank of all those who were touched by Carl and Liz.

There were many other family members who were a part of my world and made up much of the content of my work. To them, I give many thanks. All of the personalities within these pages are real and represent the richness of my life experiences.

This journey has been spotted with hardship, determination, success, failure, laughter, tears, and frustration, all of which are powerful emotions of my war within. This work is a product of the love and support given by those who have been part of my life over the years. For your parts, I again thank you.

> *To internalize your personal war within without a plan of action, will doom the combatant to merely winning small skirmishes and smoke and surface gratification vs. the satisfaction and peace of mind of winning the final battle.*
> —Ted Bagley

Preface

If there is no struggle there is no progress. Those who propose to favor freedom and yet depreciate agitation, are men who want crops without plowing up the ground. They want rain without thunder and lightning. They want the ocean's majestic waves without the awful roar of its waters.
—Fredrick Douglas

I am one who just might have a perspective that may be a bit different from yours. Though similar as we might be, we are yet undeniably different. Primarily due to significant events that shape our lives. What I have just shared with you is a perspective of my private war within. A war that not only affected my life, but the lives of millions of blacks existing in the inhumane and suffocating separatist and racist attitudes that existed in the old south. These attitudes were prevalent in the board rooms of Corporate America, in the White House, in the halls of Congress, in doctor's offices, and even in many church's in the surrounding communities.

In sharing my experiences, I am just trying to make a difference before my time is up, trying to share a thought or idea, an experience that just might help someone realize his or her life's purpose. This is a story of substantive hardships, pleasures, pain, determination, and true love, a love for those who dared to enter my dream, and touch my world in so many ways. The idea that I can make a difference, is sometimes lost in a fungus of blame and self pity. Blame of self, the system, the races, or some other passing excuse that just happened to seem plausible at that given moment. This self-pity with its highly destructive tendency is written as a sign-post and displayed at the intersection of my emotional being.

Many psychologists like Fritz Pearls and Sigmund Freud, have attempted to analyze the human development process, but none have yet found the correct ingredients or formula to bring the races together. Our final destination as human beings seems grounded in our ability to prepare for the future, effectively sustain momentum in the present, and maintain a healthy respect and understanding of the past.

The baby boomer generation, of which I am a part, is the current standard bearer. Wars have severely depleted a generation of young men who were in the most productive periods of their lives. Vietnam, Afghanistan, and Iraq have all played a major role in this saga. In addition to this fact, the baby boomers with our large knowledge base, are entering retirement with no known effective methods of transferring that knowledge to the generation x'ers. As the country moves toward a more diverse and hopefully inclusive society, we must learn to accept and respect individual differences and recognize and celebrate our similarities if the races are to survive in peace and harmony, as was intended.

This has been and will continue to be a white male dominated society. Those of us who do not fit that descriptive must not be intimidated by that fact but must reassess our commitment to excellence, stop and wiggle a bit from side to side, and settle comfortably next to our competitors where our presence will be known and respected. To accomplish that end we must be prepared for the struggle and the task ahead. Preparation is the resource that will be required to make the trip that I have just shared

Being prepared for the journey through these pages begins with a commitment to succeed. It starts with a perspective on how to reach life's goals, the extensive training required, and a zeal for a piece of life's pie. It's not just the destination that tests our altitude, but instead the journey which ultimately assumes the responsibility for raising the bar, testing our metal, and forcing us to reach for new heights. The bumps in the road are simply little life lessons that continue to whisper caution as we navigate life's highways and side roads. It's not the successes that ultimately test man's resolve, it's actually how he responds to his failures.

Ellenae L. Henry Fairhurst, president of Cumberland Chrysler-Plymouth in Fayetteville, North Carolina, put it in its proper perspective when she said, "being prepared to survive is easy, but just try being prepared for success". Mama often told us that success comes before work only in the dictionary and anything worth having is worth working for." She would say our goal should be to soar with the eagles instead of down here scratching with the chickens.

Though the old folks were unable to soar themselves because of the shackles brought on by the era, they made it perfectly clear what we were to do and where we were to go. They wanted us to make sure that we didn't set our goals at a point that underestimated and undermined our true ability. As the old saying goes, "I am not fearful of setting my goals too high and not reaching them, I am afraid that I will set them too low and accomplish them."

We must go to sleep with purpose, dream the impossible dream, and wake to the belief that our dream can become a reality. We are limited only by our ability to dream. We must develop a vision from the dream, construct an implementation plan, and work the plan against all odds. Decisions are sometimes made in segments, as it is with our lives. Those same decisions or lack there of, will have a profound effect on what we eventually become. Sometimes our desire to move ahead of the competition is inconsistent with our plan. Sometimes the sweat equity and the commitment, two key elements of the plan, are not fully developed. Sometimes our **P**reparation is not **P**rior enough to **P**revent **P**oor **P**erformance.

Introduction

A man who trims himself to suit everyone will soon whittle himself away.

—Charles Schwab

Being prepared for a journey through my life is no easy task. It starts with a true commitment to my ideals and a clear vision and focus on the future. I was brought to this work because of the many years of observing the separation that has taken place in our society among the many diverse races and cultures. This separation has resulted in poor relationships, tension, stereotyping and distrust from both sides of the racial chart. This journey must be positive, visionary, objective and honest.

It is not my intent to target any particular group or point a finger at any part of society because each time that you do point a finger, the thumb has a natural tendency to point back at you. This is really about how I have viewed the world through the eyes of someone who grew up poor and black in the Old South. The more we talk about our differences and similarities, the more understanding we will have in our life's purpose. There will be excerpts from this book that you probably will disagree with and others that will awaken in you similar events in your life. We are a part of the human race which happens to be made up of God's rainbow of colors. I do believe that red or yellow, black or white, we are precious in his sight, Jesus loves the children of the world. We are all his children. Now you can begin to see some of my religious upbringing coming into play here.

So let's get out of bed, eat some breakfast, put on your clothes and running shoes and come with me on a spirited journey through time. Please join me now on this trip to wherever it takes us. Here, in this powerful accumulation of words, is the storyteller's creed. **Let's go!!!!!!!!!!**

Chapter I

Planning the trip

Enthusiasm is the mother of effort, and without it nothing was ever accomplished.
—Ralph Waldo Emerson

Our lives are but fragile pieces of art, created piece-by piece, event-by-event, and mistake-by-mistake, which constitutes constant change to the life processes. We cannot afford to be disillusioned by the many life roadblocks both internally and externally motivated. The future, therefore, is like a blind artist who sees no paradox in the fact that their creations are unusual. How we perceive and visualize things becomes the focal points to creativity. Our art creations began as abstract pieces that start to take shape as we dream, as we perform, as we accomplish. Our changing moods, our energy and life stress points tends to drive dreams toward reality. Our ability to focus on a strategic path for ourselves, I contend, will determine our ultimate fate.

Mary Salbrig, secretary general of the World Blind Union (WBU), who lost most of her sight to macular degeneration, had a wealth of inner vision. She believed that her art improved as her sight declined. She said, "At night when my eyes are closed, I tune into a world of art where my thoughts automatically become finished paintings." Try closing your eyes and letting your imagination see the beauty that is captured there. Those who are blind are not closed to the world and their senses are sharpened by imagination which explores yet another world of beauty that we can only ponder.

We must set our sights on a visual objective which gives our lives more direction and new meaning and raises the bar on what we expect out of our life's goals. It's not just what our minds see that drives our ultimate successes it's our dreams, our thought patterns, our visions, our mental strategies that will make the difference between success and failure. As strong as this country has been in the political arena, the military superiority, the technological accomplishments and reigning world power, it is given a failure grade in human relations and the ability to mesh all cultures under one umbrella. We just can't seem to get it right. After all the years of practice, we still have issues around fair housing, voting, equal opportunity, and race relations. Why do you suppose this topic of race continues to be a wound that has not yet healed? Even with the recent election of Barack Obama as the first African American to be elected to the highest office of the land, these issues will still persist. It did prove that competence and a great plan can, even if only temporary, overcome the shackles of racism.

The country wants peace, prosperity, jobs, a trusting government, honest politicians and a secure future and it could care less who leads them back to that type environment. We have to really be careful that we don't expect too much from President Obama, after all he is just one man in the midst of major issues brought on by eight years of failure under past administrations. If blacks believe that he will make all the racism, sexism, unfair housing, poor medical care, and escalating budget deficit go away, we would be sadly mistaken. It will take as many years to repair this mess as it did to create it. What we must understand is that he is the president for all people and not just some of the people.

Greatness in any country is rooted in the soul of the nation, in its human capital. Isn't it strange that we know that fact but we either can't or won't do anything about it? Our greatness can be maximized by our pulling not only together but in the same direction. When ever this country has displayed these characteristics, the response was magnificent and everyone involved seemed to feel a homogeneous kinship to each other as in the events surrounding 911.

At a very young age, I was given a stern lesson in the difference between the races. On an artist color palette, one can mix black and white and get gray, a neutral color. There were no neutrals in the Old South. Mixing the black and white brought about red, representing the blood that was shed by both races just to get the freedom that, to this day, has eluded many people of color in what is supposed to be the land of the free and the home of the brave. The preamble to the constitution states that, "we the people" not they the people. It goes on to say, "In order to form a more perfect union, establish justice and ensure domestic tranquility. Provide for the common defense, promote the general welfare, and secure the blessings of liberty to ourselves and our posterity, do ordain and establish this Constitution for the United States of America." What has happened to the true meaning of that document? Separate but equal couldn't have been what our founding fathers intended for this nation. Then again, maybe it was.

The Gettysburg Address written by President Lincoln say "four score and seven years ago, our fathers brought fourth on this continent a new nation, conceived in liberty and dedicated to the proposition that all men are created equal." It says *ALL* men not some men. It goes on to say, "we are endowed by our creator with certain inalienable rights, that of life, liberty, and the pursuit of happiness." Who was he referring too? Was it all men or some men? Were we, men of color, considered men at all? Life, liberty, and the pursuit of happiness has been that elusive "thing" for those of us of color, before and after the four score and seven.

The 50s and 60s were very confusing times for me. I had always been taught to love and respect people based on what they do and how they behave, not who or what they were racially. Boy, how naive I was thinking that people were all the same but just came in different sizes, shapes, heights and colors. I didn't understand how individuals could have so much hate for me not because of anything that I had done but simply because of the color of my skin and the race that I was so proudly a part of.

From an external view, we were considered inferior, but why did I feel otherwise? It really took an extraordinary person to withstand hate, bigotry, and institutional racism of my era. There were many extraordinary people, both black and white, with extraordinary passion and dedication to the plight of all people. How could someone hate another, to the point of violence, strictly on the basis of skin color? For reasons beyond my comprehension at that time, our nation was sympathetic to that way of thinking, thinking that color does matter, that color did distinguish the "haves" from the "have nots", the good from the bad, success from failure, right from wrong.

An example of this hate and bigotry came from an incident that took place at a church in my home town of Birmingham Alabama. My sister Liz, being a part of the SCLC (Southern Christian Leadership Conference) under the leadership of individuals like the Rev. Ralph Abernathy, Andrew Young and the Rev. Jesse Jackson, had arranged at trip to one of the prominent white churches in the downtown area. Being as young as I was, I didn't realize that this was a part of the attempt too integrate key white establishments in the area. There were several kids my age in the group. Most of the kids were between the ages of eight and ten. I am sure that the adults felt that it would be safe to bring us to a church.

I clearly remember a particular bright sunny Sunday morning when I was standing in the living room with my Sunday clothes on. The sun rays were painting a colorful picture as it reflected off the window pane in our living room. Mother was in the kitchen cooking her famous biscuits, bacon and eggs and the aroma filled my nostrils with delight as I anticipated the morning meal. There was always a jar of apple butter on the table to compliment those hot biscuits. This was a perfect morning and I was proud of being the first one ready for church and I didn't need any help even with tying my tie. Back in the day, parents thought it was cute to dress us boys in a bow tie and short pants. Not me, I wanted a long tie with long pants primarily to cover my skinny legs. I know I have started to digress a bit but those Sunday mornings were truly special. Just as I was about to ask for a sample of those hot biscuits, my sister came into my room and asked if I wanted to go with her to church. It was somewhat of a strange request because we always got up on Sunday to attend church. Little did I know that this would be a new chapter in my personal war within.

I look out of the picture window in our living room and saw two shiny black cars sitting in front of the house. There were at least three people sitting in the cars and my sister had gone outside to talk to them. Pretty soon she returned to the house and asked if I was ready. "Ready for what," I said to my self. Who were these people and what did they have to do with our going to church? I had not yet had a bite of those biscuits. I asked Liz about the people in the front of the house and she looked at me as if to say shut up and come on, so I did with my stomach still growling from hunger. Mother yelled out, "That boy has not eaten yet, where are you going?" "Mama, don't worry about him, I will get him something later, we will be late if we don't leave now," Liz replied.

If Mother and Daddy had known what we were about to do, they would have had a fit. As I slid into that big car, the conversation was about civil rights and what their next moves would be. All I could think about was Bill eating my portion of breakfast. He and I would sometimes have a contest to see who could eat the most biscuits. Daddy would look at us and shake his head in disbelief. Now, we stay away from bread because it adds inches to our waste lines; we don't eat too many eggs because of our cholesterol; we don't drink too much caffeine because of our nerves; we stay away from red meat because it stays in our systems too long; the apple butter that we once ate has to much sugar and sugar adds weight. Boy whatever happened to the old days. Someone bring them back please.

What were civil rights anyway and what did it have to do with church? As we drove out of the community, I couldn't help but notice that this was definitely not our normal route to church. I asked, "Liz where were we going?" She said that we were going to visit another church in the downtown area. It seemed as if we had been driving forever and I was suppressing the urge to ask that age old kids question, "Are we there yet". It seemed as if we had been driving forever when we approached this large building that looked more like a big department store or sports arena than a church. It was slowly becoming obvious to me that this was not going to be our normal routine or what I was use to on Sunday morning. As we parked in the parking lot across from the church, we were the immediate subject of some very uncomfortable stares and whispers from a few passers by. There were two men and one woman in our group other than Liz and me. As we approached the church, I could see that a crowd was beginning to gather at the front of the church. Were we the subject of their attention? What was going on? Had there been an accident or was someone sick? As we walked closer and closer, I could all but hear the heart beats of those in our group and this was beginning to feel very uncomfortable even to a small fry like me. As we started to climb the stairs to the church, a voice from one of the white men standing on the top step yelled out, "What do you people want," he asked, "and where do you think you are going?"

One of the men in our group spoke up and said that we were there to participate in the Sunday services and that we didn't want any trouble. Well we may not have wanted any trouble but trouble wanted us. Suddenly, the group of white men and women started to laugh. "You are here to do what?" he asked? The man with us again stated, "we just wanted to join in the services and listen to God's word, nothing else." One very vocal and mean spirited white man started to approach us and pointed his finger saying, "not here you are not, so get your asses off this property." His words shocked me because Mother and Daddy never spoke like that.

When the large, fat and hateful white man saw that the men in our group were not moving, he stopped and shook his fist at us. By this time there were police coming up to the church from all directions. Evidently, someone from the church had called them. I was confused because the good book says "who so ever will let them come and hear the word of God." That's what my Daddy always told us. For the first time I thought there had to be more than one God because they did not want us to worship with them. As the police approached, one of the men in our group told the officer we didn't want any trouble. We were there in peace and wanted to worship which was our right. Even the police seemed angry that we were there and sided with white church members. Why did they have their billy-clubs drawn and why were they talking so mean to us? A few of them were also laughing which seemed a little strange to me. I was always taught that the law was there to protect us. Why were they supporting these hateful people? Why didn't they want us there? What was it about us that brought about this radical reaction?

The police began to push us back from the steps with their billy-Clubs while telling us to leave or be thrown in jail. Wow!, Thrown in jail for wanting to worship the Lord? Now, I was really confused. One of the men in our group asked why they were treating us that way. He said that we had a right to be there. Another of the men in our group said that it was no use staying any longer where we were not wanted and motioned for us to follow him away from the church.

As the men in our group led us away "we sang, we shall overcome, we shall over come, we shall over come some day, deep in my heart, I do believe that we shall over come someday." Little did I know then, that song would become the battle cry of the civil rights movement and a thorn in the ears of the oppressors. As the police escorted us to our cars, I looked back to see what those alleged Christians were doing. They had quickly turned into a nasty mob. They did not see us as equals. In fact, they choose not to see or deal with us at all. It was as if, we were invisible. The police were supposed to be "Peace Officers" but there was no peace to be found on that Sunday.

As we arrived at our cars that disappointing Sunday morning, I was starting to experience the beginning of my war within. Why were they so hateful to us? Why didn't they want us there? Did they have a different God that was specifically for white folks? Why did they call the police, we weren't doing anything wrong. Why, why, why? While I thought about the normal ways that the church would operate, the adults on both sides were dealing with a more pressing issue, that of race and human rights. There was not even relief from the shackles of racism in God's church. Now I am thinking, if we can't have peace at church, where could we find it. I was young but it did not escape me that the faces of the men and women on the church steps showed intense hate, and indifference to a people simply because of race. It disappointed me because I wanted to see what the inside of the white folks church looked like. Was it the same as ours? Did they have a picture of the Lord's Supper hanging on the wall as we had in our church? Did they have a good choir? Did the preacher preach fire and brimstone as ours did? Would they have refreshments in the basement after church as we did? I was thinking about all of the important stuff. At that point in my life, I could not imagine just how significant the actions at the church would be to my personal war within.

On the ride back home, I asked Liz why were they so hateful toward us? She said that I would understand when I was older.

Little did she know it but I was beginning to understand right at that moment in front of that church. I knew that we were the only black folks, so it had to be because of us. Even the so called police protection was showing their bias toward our race. The very people that we looked to for law and order were themselves pawns in the hate game and willing to suppress a people simple because of difference. We knew what side of the scale we were on. Being on the wrong side of the tracks was a motivator to most of us to fight a little harder, dig a little deeper and seek even higher ground. To be different should be a blessing of God's diverse universe. To be hateful and raciest is a stain that even Tide, Cheer or bleach all together could not remove.

A group of more than 900 children were arrested over a period of time simply because they were demonstrating for equal rights. The situation had become incendiary. The inhumane treatment, the dogs, the fire hoses, and the hate ravaged environment finally raised the consciousness of the nation and caused the President of the United States, President Kennedy, to send a civil rights bill to Congress and to use the National Guard to curb the unrest. These actions on the part of the Birmingham Police Department ushered in an era that saw attacks on people of color using fire hoses, police dogs and cattle prods. To watch this inhumane treatment by officials of the law added fuel to the fire that was burning inside me. A fire to withstand racism, a fire to make things better for me and my family and a fire to never have that slave or victim mentality that Daddy often talked about.

Just after the highly successful "March on Washington" and King's famous "I Have a Dream" speech, four little black school girls were killed when a bomb exploded as they attended church at the Sixteenth Street Baptist Church in downtown Birmingham. One of the girls was the daughter of my teacher, Mrs. McNair. Her name was Denise McNair, a beautiful and gifted young lady with what could have been a bright future, never got the opportunity to share in the dream, to showcase her talents, to make a difference. Her death was not in vain. Many like Denise gave their lives for the cause, for the dream. It would have been so easy to hate those who were responsible but our parents taught us to pray for those who seek to hurt you and forgive as the bible teaches. Back then I found that pretty hard, but as I got older, I started to realize that we had to learn to love even those who chose not to love us back.

No person has the right to take another life. God gave it and only God should take it away. Those responsible for the bombings saw themselves as protectors of a way of life whose time had passed. These events were just a few of many that were to take place in our communities by these cowards. Nights were a time to worry and hope that the darkness would not bring more tragedy. Under the cover of night, white hate groups would come with their home made bombs and blasting caps with the aim to destroy all blacks who stood in their way. They would first plant a decoy bomb with a timer set to explode in the early morning hours, just as many were getting up for morning breakfast. The initial bomb would draw people from their homes because of their curiosity. As individuals gathered around the location of the first bomb, a carefully planned second explosion would occur approximately ten to fifteen minutes after the first. The second explosion consisted of a large amount of explosive, metals like nails, and other piercing objects used to kill or injure.

Those incidents are indicative of the gap that was ever present between the races. Not only were we not liked and appreciated by some of the opposite race, we often didn't treat each other with the respect and dignity that we were so desperately seeking. When there were riots, we burned our own community and looted our own small businesses. Why I couldn't understand. I can understand the frustration that builds as people struggle economically but to take it out on innocent people in that manner was a disgrace.

I remember a time when I returned to the old community to celebrate my high school reunion. The guys that didn't like me then still did not like me but couldn't remember why. After all those years, they couldn't remember why they didn't, but they were convinced that they didn't. As it is with hate, it eats away at the fabric of a society primarily without reason. Hate not only destroys the hated, it destroys the hater. It affects the family, the children, and the overall relationship equation. That didn't seem to matter in the Old South. All that mattered was that the races were to remain separate . . . . period.

Our community's became little war zones where those who were in power would use that power to harass and dehumanize those who just wanted to be a part of society. A society that our forefathers and mothers helped to built with sweat equity, struggle and sacrifice, one where we could look to improve its conditions for our children and their children and one where the lion could lay down with the lamb in peace and harmony. That is the imagination that I talked about earlier and that's the world that I wanted to be a part of.

Destroying the few upscale, more progressive communities of blacks, seemed to be the objective of hate groups like the KKK. What they learned very quickly was that the faith and the resolve of a people would endure adversity, bigotry, and hate. We were not going to be victimized by hooded cowards who were afraid to be recognized. These hooded thugs were men who must have had low self-esteem because why else would they fear a people who had no economic power, no political clout and very little ability to challenge them in any socio-economic way.

So why, I kept asking myself, would men of stature and prominence in and around Birmingham commit acts of terror and mayhem against an innocent people? They had families and responsibilities just as our parents did, so why, why, why? The answer kept coming back saying it was because of hate bigotry and fear. Fear of the unknown, a fear of the loss of their way of life, the fear of having to share what was our God-given rights. This cancer was, and still is, a disease for which society has yet to find a cure. Its like the dam that has cracks in it, you can patch it for only so long before the pressure of the water behind the dam attacks its weakest point and the dam eventually breaks. As it was with people of color, the racism, bigotry and down right disrespect finally caused the dam to break, resulting in demonstrations and riots all over the south.

To protect our communities from these unwarranted attacks and continued harassment, our fathers formed watch committees to cover the gates and entries into our neighborhoods. After many hours working on hard labor jobs in the sweat shops of Birmingham's steel and iron ore foundries, chicken processing plants, and the railroads, they would sacrifice their rest periods for our safety by standing at the entries to our neighborhoods with any weapons they could find, protecting us from the racists that were so cowardly that they would spread their hatred under the cover of darkness and behind sheets to protect their identity. Only slimy things tend to come out after dark. They act like bats, opossum, and other critters that choose the night to do their wandering. They scavenge, pillage, and destroy while others are asleep. They spread their garbage and return to the wet, damp, dark rocks that they hide under during the day. Those rocks were located where you lease expected them to be. Their rocks were the police force, political arenas, law offices, and even judge's chambers of our cities.

On rare occasions, I would go with mother and some of the other neighborhood women to take snacks and coffee to the men protecting our community and would hang around long enough to hear them tell wonderful stories about their childhood experiences as well as the racist encounters they were subjected to on a daily basis. The thing that impressed me most was their ability to laugh under those pressing circumstances. It's not what happens to you that sets the standard, it's how you respond that makes the difference. Martin Luther King preached none violence and as a people we listened. The problem was, those who sought to harm us didn't.

In spite of their adversity, our fathers were strong, self made men who refused to give in to the hate-laced environment in Birmingham and the surrounding cities. They were men who thought and believed that being poor was a socio-economic condition not a state of mind. They believed that just because their pockets were empty didn't mean that their families would go hungry. They believed that life was what you made it and not what it made you.

My father often told us that if we felt like slaves we would become what our thought patterns dictated. Act like a slave, think like a slave, and become a slave. We were taught to meet people on our terms and not theirs. My parents would say that respect is earned, one encounter at a time. We were told to maintain our values and integrity for they were all we really owned. They instilled in us the desire, hope and will to succeed. We were told that education was the key to our being able to realize these ends even though the times made it difficult for them to realize the same end. That teaching must have worked because each one of us got our piece of the pie as did many of our family members. Liz was a professor at Alabama State University for a great number of years before her passing. Bill was manager at General Motors in the Engineering Department of the Electric Car Division prior to his retirement and well . . . little old me did manage to make it to the Vice Presidents ranks of many large corporations and remain in that position today. Not bad for off springs of parents who never realized their potential or who didn't finish off their slice of life's pie.

Yes, these were indeed men and women light years ahead of their time in understanding what it took to succeed in an opportunity-starved environment. They just didn't have the tools or support to make their dreams become a reality. Their advanced thoughts and ideas were concealed and placed in hibernation simply because of the color of their skin and certainly not because of the content of their character. What a travesty that such creativity, talent, and individual skills were never to be realized under that Jim Crow era. Their talents were obvious, but recognition for that talent was not to be realized. Those were trying times that tended to test the will to survive and the soul of a people. My individual burning within had begun with a great deal of confusion yet anticipation. I yearned to be a part of the changes that just had to come. Things just could not continue as they were. Change had to start soon.

From a vantage point of the 1990's, it became increasingly difficult to remember the more forbidding world of yesterday, a world of "separate but never equal." A world where we struggled just to survive and one in transition from the days of Ala. Governor George Wallace, and Birmingham Police Commissioner T. Eugene Bull Connor who supported Jim Crow laws, and attacks on civil rights at the legislative level.

Many of you are not familiar with the impact that these Jim Crow laws had on black people. Consider these facts obtained from the Martin Luther King, Jr., National historic site Interpretive Staff.

From the 1880s to the 1960s, a majority of American states enforced segregation through "Jim Crow" laws. From Delaware to California, and from North Dakota to Texas, many states (and cities, too) could impose legal punishments on people for consorting with members of another race. The most common types of laws forbade intermarriage and ordered business owners and public institutions to keep their black and white clientele separated.

Here is a sampling of laws from various states:

Nurses No person or corporation shall require any white female nurse to nurse in wards or rooms in hospitals, either public or private, in which Negro men are placed. (*Alabama*)

Buses—All passenger stations in this state operated by any motor transportation company shall have separate waiting rooms or space and separate ticket windows for the white and colored races. (*Alabama*)

Railroads—The conductor of each passenger train is authorized and required to assign each passenger to the car or the division of the car, when it is divided by a partition, designated for the race to which such passenger belongs. (*Alabama*)

Restaurants—It shall be unlawful to conduct a restaurant or other place for the serving of food in the city, at which white and colored people are served in the same room, unless such white and colored persons are effectually separated by a solid partition extending from the floor upward to a distance of seven feet or higher, and unless a separate entrance from the street is provided for each compartment. (*Alabama*)

Pool and Billiard Rooms—It shall be unlawful for a Negro and white person to play together or in company with each other at any game of pool or billiards. (*Alabama*)

Toilet Facilities, Male Every employer of white or Negro males shall provide for such white or Negro males reasonably accessible and separate toilet facilities. (*Alabama*)

Intermarriage—The marriage of a person of Caucasian blood with a Negro, Mongolian, Malay, or Hindu shall be null and void. (*Arizona*)

Intermarriage All marriages between a white person and a Negro, or between a white person and a person of Negro descent to the fourth generation inclusive, are hereby forever prohibited. (*Florida*)

Cohabitation Any negro man and white woman, or any white man and negro woman, who are not married to each other, who shall habitually live in and occupy in the nighttime the same room shall each be punished by imprisonment not exceeding twelve (12) months, or by fine not exceeding five hundred ($500.00) dollars. (*Florida*)

Education The schools for white children and the schools for Negro children shall be conducted separately. (*Florida*)

Juvenile Delinquents There shall be separate buildings, not nearer than one fourth mile to each other, one for white boys and one for Negro boys. White boys and Negro boys shall not, in any manner, be associated together or worked together. (*Florida*)

Mental Hospitals The Board of Control shall see that proper and distinct apartments are arranged for said patients, so that in no case shall Negroes and white persons be together. (*Georgia*)

Intermarriage It shall be unlawful for a white person to marry anyone except a white person. Any marriage in violation of this section shall be void. (*Georgia*)

Barbers No colored barber shall serve as a barber [to] white women or girls. (*Georgia*)

Burial The officer in charge shall not bury, or allow to be buried, any colored persons upon ground set apart or used for the burial of white persons. (*Georgia*)

Restaurants All persons licensed to conduct a restaurant, shall serve either white people exclusively or colored people exclusively and shall not sell to the two races within the same room or serve the two races anywhere under the same license. (*Georgia*)

Amateur Baseball It shall be unlawful for any amateur white baseball team to play baseball on any vacant lot or baseball diamond within two blocks of a playground devoted to the Negro race, and it shall be unlawful for any amateur colored baseball team to play baseball in any vacant lot or baseball diamond within two blocks of any playground devoted to the white race. (*Georgia*)

Parks It shall be unlawful for colored people to frequent any park owned or maintained by the city for the benefit, use and enjoyment of white persons . . . and unlawful for any white person to frequent any park owned or maintained by the city for the use and benefit of colored persons. (*Georgia*)

Wine and Beer All persons licensed to conduct the business of selling beer or wine . . . shall serve either white people exclusively or colored people exclusively and shall not sell to the two races within the same room at any time. (*Georgia*)

Reform Schools The children of white and colored races committed to the houses of reform shall be kept entirely separate from each other. (*Kentucky*)

Circus Tickets All circuses, shows, and tent exhibitions, to which the attendance of . . . more than one race is invited or expected to attend shall provide for the convenience of its patrons not less than two ticket offices with individual ticket sellers, and not less than two entrances to the said performance, with individual ticket takers and receivers, and in the case of outside or tent performances, the said ticket offices shall not be less than twenty-five (25) feet apart. (*Louisiana*)

Housing Any person . . . who shall rent any part of any such building to a negro person or a negro family when such building is already in whole or in part in occupancy by a white person or white family, or vice versa when the building is in occupancy by a negro person or negro family, shall be guilty of a misdemeanor and on conviction thereof shall be punished by a fine of not less than twenty-five ($25.00) nor more than one hundred ($100.00) dollars or be imprisoned not less than 10, or more than 60 days, or both such fine and imprisonment in the discretion of the court. (*Louisiana*)

The Blind The board of trustees shall . . . maintain a separate building . . . on separate ground for the admission, care, instruction, and support of all blind persons of the colored or black race. (*Louisiana*)

Intermarriage All marriages between a white person and a negro, or between a white person and a person of Negro descent, to the third generation, inclusive, or between a white person and a member of the Malay race; or between the Negro and a member of the Malay race; or between a person of Negro descent, to the third generation, inclusive, and a member of the Malay race, are forever prohibited, and shall be void. (*Maryland*)

Railroads All railroad companies and corporations, and all persons running or operating cars or coaches by steam on any railroad line or track in the State of Maryland, for the transportation of passengers, are hereby required to provide separate cars or coaches for the travel and transportation of the white and colored passengers. (*Maryland*)

Education Separate schools shall be maintained for the children of the white and colored races. (*Mississippi*)

Promotion of Equality Any person . . . who shall be guilty of printing, publishing or circulating printed, typewritten or written matter urging or presenting for public acceptance or general information, arguments or suggestions in favor of social equality or of intermarriage between whites and negroes, shall be guilty of a misdemeanor and subject to fine or not exceeding five hundred

(500.00) dollars or imprisonment not exceeding six (6) months or both. (*Mississippi*)

Intermarriage The marriage of a white person with a Negro or mulatto or person who shall have one-eighth or more of negro blood, shall be unlawful and void. (*Mississippi*)

Hospital Entrances There shall be maintained by the governing authorities of every hospital maintained by the state for treatment of white and colored patients separate entrances for white and colored patients and visitors, and such entrances shall be used by the race only for which they are prepared. (*Mississippi*)

Prisons The warden shall see that the white convicts shall have separate apartments for both eating and sleeping from the negro convicts. (*Mississippi*)

Education Separate free schools shall be established for the education of children of African descent; and it shall be unlawful for any colored child to attend any white school, or any white child to attend a colored school. (*Missouri*)

Intermarriage All marriages between . . . white persons and Negroes or white persons and Mongolians . . . are prohibited and declared absolutely void . . . No person having one-eighth part or more of Negro blood shall be permitted to marry any white person, nor shall any white person be permitted to marry any Negro or person having one-eighth part or more of negro blood. (*Missouri*)

Education Separate rooms [shall] be provided for the teaching of pupils of African descent, and [when] said rooms are so provided, such pupils may not be admitted to the school rooms occupied and used by pupils of Caucasian or other descent. (*New Mexico*)

Textbooks Books shall not be interchangeable between the white and colored schools, but shall continue to be used by the race first using them. (*North Carolina*)

Libraries The state librarian is directed to fit up and maintain a separate place for the use of the colored people who may come to the library for the purpose of reading books or periodicals. (*North Carolina*)

Militia The white and colored militia shall be separately enrolled, and shall never be compelled to serve in the same organization. No organization of colored troops shall be permitted where white troops are available, and while white permitted to be organized, colored troops shall be under the command of white officers. (*North Carolina*)

Transportation The . . . Utilities Commission . . . is empowered and directed to require the establishment of separate waiting rooms at all stations for the white and colored races. (*North Carolina*)

Teaching Any instructor who shall teach in any school, college or institution where members of the white and colored race are received and enrolled as pupils for instruction shall be deemed guilty of a misdemeanor, and upon conviction thereof, shall be fined in any sum not less than ten dollars ($10.00) nor more than fifty dollars ($50.00) for each offense. (*Oklahoma*)

Fishing, Boating, and Bathing The [Conservation] Commission shall have the right to make segregation of the white and colored races as to the exercise of rights of fishing, boating and bathing. (*Oklahoma*)

Mining The baths and lockers for the Negroes shall be separate from the white race, but may be in the same building. (*Oklahoma*)

Telephone Booths The Corporation Commission is hereby vested with power and authority to require telephone companies . . . to maintain separate booths for white and colored patrons when there is a demand for such separate booths. The Corporation Commission shall determine the necessity for said separate booths only upon complaint of the people in the town and vicinity to be served after due hearing as now provided by law in other complaints filed with the Corporation Commission. (*Oklahoma*)

Lunch Counters No persons, firms, or corporations, who or which furnish meals to passengers at station restaurants or station eating houses, in times limited by common carriers of said passengers, shall furnish said meals to white and colored passengers in the same room, or at the same table, or at the same counter. (*South Carolina*)

Child Custody It shall be unlawful for any parent, relative, or other white person in this State, having the control or custody of any white child, by right of guardianship, natural or acquired, or otherwise, to dispose of, give or surrender such white child permanently into the custody, control, maintenance, or support, of a Negro. (*South Carolina*)

Libraries Any white person of such county may use the county free library under the rules and regulations prescribed by the Commissioners court and may be entitled to all the privileges thereof. Said court shall make proper provision for the Negroes of said county to be served through a separate branch or branches of the county free library, which shall be administered by [a] custodian of the Negro race under the supervision of the county librarian. (*Texas*)

Education [The County Board of Education] shall provide schools of two kinds; those for white children and those for colored children. (*Texas*)

Theaters Every person ... operating ... any public hall, theatre, opera house, motion picture show or any place of public entertainment or public assemblage which is attended by both white and colored persons, shall separate the white race and the colored race and shall set apart and designate ... certain seats therein to be occupied by white persons and a portion thereof, or certain seats therein, to be occupied by colored persons. (*Virginia*)

Railroads The conductors or managers on all such railroads shall have power, and are hereby required, to assign to each white or colored passenger his or her respective car, coach or compartment. If the passenger fails to disclose his race, the conductor and managers, acting in good faith, shall be the sole judges of his race. (*Virginia*)

Intermarriage All marriages of white persons with Negroes, Mulattos, Mongolians, or Malaya hereafter contracted in the State of Wyoming are and shall be illegal and void. (*Wyoming*)

Just imagine how difficult it was to have to operate and live under degradation as displayed at that time. It was a world scarred by injustice and hatred and one deeply tainted by prejudice and cowardly acts committed by hooded thugs, afraid to show their true identities. Little did we know at the time that many of the hooded cowards were prominent citizens, doctors, lawyers, politicians, policemen, and others who were responsible for criminal acts against innocent people? They hid under the umbrella of groups such as the Ku Klux Klan and John Birch Society.

These racist groups pioneered the encoding of implicit cultural forms of white racism and Christian nationalist Anti-Semitism rather than relying on the white supremacist biological determinism and open criticism of Jews that had typified the old right prior to WWII. The Society's anti-communism and states rights libertarianism was based on sincere principles, but it clearly served as a cover for organizing by segregationists and white supremacists. How much of this was conscious, and how much unconscious, is difficult to determine. That the Birch Society clearly attracted members with a more hate-filled (even fascistic) agenda is undeniable, and these more zealous elements used the JBS as a recruitment pool from which to draw persons toward a more radical stance on issues of race and culture (information about the John Birch Society was obtained from the Political Resource Association).

John Johnson, publisher of Ebony Magazine, put it in its proper perspective, "we believed in 1945, that black Americans needed positive images in their lives to help us focus on what could be instead of what was". Our role models back in the day were our principals and teachers. Though we had black professionals in other fields like lawyers, doctors, engineers, even policemen, they were relegated to operating in their neighborhoods only. They had to "stay in their places", if they were going to be allowed to keep their businesses.

We believe then, and still do, that that we have to change images before you can change acts and institutions. My story deals with two such images. One that others had of us as a race and as individuals, and the other reflecting how we felt about ourselves. These images took us on a long roller coaster ride of higher than high highs, and lower than low lows. Fortunately there was Dr. Martin Luther King, Jr. and James Brown. Yes, I said James Brown, who helped us regain our footing as black people when he wrote the song, "Say it loud, I'm black and I'm proud." Until James and Martin came along, we were putting away our black dolls and processing our hair to look more like the whites. James even did the processing thing himself. Maybe he thought that it made him more acceptable to whites in the entertainment industry. Many blacks felt that they needed to look and act like the more successful whites to be accepted and experience success themselves. Pride, dignity, self-esteem, and self-confidence were much needed attributes.

As the country grew through an amazing technological period including state-of-the-art manufacturing, robotics, global competition between powerful nations, and leading-edge research, our piece of the pie grew smaller and smaller as a direct result of the imaging process. Some of these images were self-inflicted, while others were legislated based on political tom-foolery of the times. The surface of the nation seemed to grow stronger while the inner-core grew substantially weaker as a result of a calculated elimination of a capable and talented resource, people of color.

The periods covered in my journey through time were those securely marked by measures of despair and hopelessness that was rampant in Black America. Our lives were severely impacted and impaired by the suffocating grip of separatism and segregation. It was an era that saw few opportunities for blacks in the halls of the legislative arena. There were very few people of color represented in the mayor's offices, senate chambers, judges' benches, and board rooms. Yes, we own our businesses but only those within our communities and those have little impact on the economic conditions of our people. Prices are required to be too high and inventory levels too low to compete with the larger more well resourced and sophisticated majority businesses. Entrepreneurial aspirations were far and few in our communities.

Economically, we were unable to borrow money when we had none. It took us a while to understand a system that required you to have money in order to borrow money. We paid more for housing and services than did any other culture. We had less medical treatment, less money, less insurance, fewer jobs and bottom line, less everything which was the plight of our community and which fed the flames of my personal war within.

The color line was still drawn in major league sports. Blacks appeared sparingly in the national media and when we were featured it was usually in an unflattering manner that more than occasionally failed to offer a hint of the breadth and depth of our abilities and the real richness of the black heritage. People of the opposite race chose to see us as being more like JJ of "Good Times" or King Fish of "The Amos and Andy" fame rather than Bill Cosby and Felicia Rashad of the "Huxtables" (a TV family where both parents were professionals). This was institutionalized racism at its finest.

Because of the wide distribution of households with televisions, the media tended to set public opinion; create images whether good or bad with ratings accumulated through electronic boxes placed throughout the country in homes of the consumers. Isn't it strange that these rating boxes seem to never make it to the black households? If you don't believe me, just ask any black person that you know whether there has ever been a box placed in their homes. There has to be blacks participating somewhere, but where? These images were changing, though grudgingly. For every one step we made, two were taken away. We now own businesses, run major corporations, excel in sports, manage hospitals, try cases in the top courts in the land but we still are not considered equal. With all the progress, unfortunately racism remains a cancer that, even today, is left unchecked in our society. It, unfortunately, has prevented a great nation from becoming even greater. We continue to maintain our hopes and dreams through the muck and morrowed clay of this inhuman social cesspool that continues to pull us down.

We could still feel the winds of change whispering the tune, "Hold on to God's unchanging hand". We were encouraged by our elders to tie a knot in the rope of life and hold on as tightly as we could. Our religion was our refuge and somehow our trust in God seemed to make things all right and as the Rev. Jesse Jackson would say, "Keep hope alive". The war within kept us going. Where there was despair, we had hope, when the world thought that we were asleep, we were dreaming of a better day, when thugs and cowards knocked us down we continued to get up. These were times that we were redefining our purpose, understanding our heritage and preparing our tools for the journey.

Dr. Martin Luther King, Jr. said, "Men hate each other because they fear each other, they fear each other because they don't know each other, and they don't know each other because they are so often separated from each other." There was no way for whites and blacks to have a common bond because the color line was drawn wide and deep and the line of demarcation was not to be broken. In every Southern community, the races were separated by the railroad tracks. White folks lived on one side of the tracks and we lived on the other. That was the way things were.

The traditions of our society have been so set and crystallized that many social, political, and educational obstacles stand like giant red oaks in the way of real change and real racial fusion. In order that we all survive, this fusion must take place collectively, socially, spiritually, economically and universally. It must be overt and colorless and above all *IT JUST MUST BE!*

Chapter II

The Beginning

> Life is an eternal struggle to keep one's earning capacity up to one's yearning capacity.
>
> —*Milwaukee Farm Workers*

Birmingham, Alabama was a town with a spotted history of racial indifference. Its air was tainted with a blue haze of summer and the smell of red clay and Iron Ore. There was almost always a fine mist that hovered over the city like the smoke from mama's old Kenmore stove. This city in Alabama, with its legacy stained by the blood of many of its black and white citizens who were not satisfied with the way things were, was the backdrop for the turmoil that I was experiencing earlier in my life.

There are still vivid memories of the police dogs, Jim Crow laws, the Ku Klux Klan, demonstrations, prayer meetings, neighborhood bombings, and senseless murders of the weak and the innocent. These incident had personal impact on me. How could life mean so little to those who were trying to preserve an era that had long since passed? This hideous event along with other cross burning and shooting incidents served to fuel my personal war within.

I can still envision, in that little sleepy town called Titusville, Mama jumping from the top step of that old tattered double tenant house with a panic stricken expression on her face because her four year old (me), even then, did not know the meaning of fear. Those of you who were born with a silver spoon in your mouth probably don't know what a double tenant house is. It's a dwelling in which two families lived. The structure, though one building, is divided in half with a single family living on each side. Normally, they are three room homes with a kitchen, a sleeping room, and a living room. These were rental units because in that day, very few families could afford to own their own home.

It was my normal routine to play in our backyard on a make-shift swing constructed from an old tire and rope hanging over an oak tree limb like spaghetti straps on an evening gown. You may notice that I didn't say my mother's evening gown. Back in the day, my Mother didn't have an evening gown and there were no formal events for blacks to go to anyway, at least not in that community. The only meetings that the parents were involved in were PTA or teacher conferences or the principle's office where my brother and sister usually would end up. You notice that I didn't say me.

The back yard was our refuge and most of our activities took place. My big brother Bill, or "little Bru" as most called him, being even more sneaky and mischievous than I was, did not hesitate to push me higher and harder in that old makeshift swing, thinking nothing of the impending danger. As I look back on that particular incident, I am sure now that Bill knew exactly what was about to happen and was looking forward to the eventual outcome. Liz, our older and self-proclaimed "smarter" sister, had warned us about playing around that old tree but we were having too much fun to have it spoiled by some old girl anyway. At that moment, as the swing was at the apex, that old tire started to shake and move closer and closer, with each push, to that tree which had to have been growing there for at least a hundred years from the size of that old thing.

Bill, realizing the swing was about to crash, made a half-hearted attempt to grab me. I, being naive, could not see what was about to happen, yelled for him to let me go. What a time for him to start listening to me. My yelling came to an abrupt end when the old rope seemed to explode sending me and the tire through the air directly into that old tree. Just as I hit the tree and let out the loudest scream ever imagined, Mama arrived on the scene. Dazed and bruises, I crawled into her arms. I was more ruffled by the laughter coming from Bill and Liz, who could be heard saying, "I told you so, I told you so. You just don't know how to quit." Mama, having made sure that I was all right, began to scold the two for letting it happen. With a smile and a smirk, I was carried off in the graceful arms of Mama leaving Bill and Liz to ponder their strategy of getting even with me for Mama's scolding.

Mother always seemed so wonderful and larger than life to me. She stood 5 feet 5 inches tall with a personality that could soothe the soul of the most savage beast. She was a strong and dedicated wife and mother with ties directly to God himself. She always encouraged us to be the best we could be. All that she asked was that we give it our best effort. If we came up short with maximum effort, she was satisfied. With minimal education, Mama was smarter than many of the so-called educated people that I have come in contact with over the years. I can still hear her say "Book sense must be accompanied by good common sense." She was the nail in the edifice that always managed to keep the foundation of the family intact.

Then there was Daddy who as we would say, was definitely a piece of work. He was small in stature but never-the-less a self made proud, strong, opinionated man. He had a mind like a steel trap, with a detailed memory which was quite astonishing. He was the master of the phrase "when I was your age, I knew better than to do what you crazy kids will do. My parents would tear me up." We would say, under our breath of course, so that it could not be heard, "when you were our age, the world was brand new." Children think of their parents as antiques who are out of touch with reality. That has not changed as I raise my own children. I now realize that the generation at hand and the significant events of this new generation will shape their beliefs well beyond that which history has provided. My role has changed with my children from one of being the disciplinarian, to one of coach and counselor, as they have grown out of the teenage years. Those parents who fail to make the transition will risk losing the trust and security of the parent-child relationship and force them into independence prematurely.

I will not say that our Daddy was an affectionate man, but we always knew that he loved us through the continuous sacrifices he made to give us the basic requirements. He was a no-nonsense individual who expected excellence in anything we tried. I can remember clearly, one particular occasion, when I was participating in a track meet at Legion Field, one of the few places blacks had for sporting events in Birmingham. I knew that I was good and one of the most talented athletes in my school in track and had no reason to practice like the others. After all, during the regular track season, I had defeated most of my competition with little problem. Dad had often warned us that hard work can overcome talent on a given day but who was paying attention to those old proverbs.

On the Saturday morning of the track meet, I was standing at the starting line of the hundred yard dash just pondering my actions after what I knew would be a win for me. The starter's gun soon sounded and I was off like a flash, as I had done so often in the past. At the 50 yard marker, things were going true to form. At the 60 yard marker I thought it was the appropriate time for me to "HOT DOG" a bit and look back to see just how far the others were behind me. My dream became a nightmare when not one but two of my competitors passed me just before the finish line. I had beaten both at previous meets during the season. Not only was I humiliated by the disappointing finish, but now I had to face Daddy. My best bet would have been to just keep running right out of the stadium. The look of "I TOLD YOU SO" was written all over his face. He could not stomach my losing because of poor preparation. Because Daddy believed in teaching you a lesson for not listening, my punishment was to walk the approximate seven miles home with a full bag of equipment while he followed at a distance in the family car, to ensure that no one bothered me or give me a ride.

On another somewhat similar occasion, I was participating in our normal neighborhood baseball game with many of the kids in the community. I was known to be one of the best at baseball among the kids. During one of the innings, a ball was hit toward me in left field by Junior Belcher, another good player. With my speed and quickness and a little "hot dog", I was off at the crack of the ball hitting the bat. It was hit so hard that I only had a few seconds to race back, take a quick look in the direction of the ball, and at the last minute, leap against the fence to make a spectacular catch. I felt proud of myself because I had saved the game for my team. As I jogged back from the outfield to receive the congratulations from my teammates, I could see Daddy who had dropped by the park to observe. He always had this steel piercing look about him when there was a lesson to be delivered. I was smiling as I ran toward him to get his support and to hear a word of praise. Boy, how wrong I was. All he said was, "boy, you think that you did something great? If you had not been out of position and trying to be so flashy and hot dogging out there, you wouldn't have had to leap to make that catch." My great moment was dashed by those few words coming from one of the hardest graders in all of creation. My teachers didn't grade as hard as Daddy. He was indeed a piece of work.

Those were hard but necessary lessons about life. Nothing was to be given to you in this life, you had to earn it. Think through things that are facing you and be prepared to address it in the most effective manner. Though you may master one obstacle, there was another awaiting you around the next corner or over the next hill. I was proud of what I had done but that old man knew that the fundamentals of the game were more important than one spectacular catch. His message was that we can't survive on talent alone. We must understand what position we want to play in life and give it our best. We must combine our God given talents with our cognitive ability. Those were hard lessons that you sometimes don't get the true meaning of until later in life.

These were lessons that over the years I have shared with other young people with whom I have come in contact and shared some form of mentoring relationship. One such individual was Sasha Mukerjee, a neighbor's child whose family was from India. He is a young man now, but credits the track and baseball stories I had shared with him with contributing to his success in the business world. He is a manager in one of the larger industries in the Atlanta area. He also manages his own business.

I will never forget the night that Sasha and Ashu, his brother, rang our door bell in the middle of the night because their father was having breathing problems. I quickly got out of bed put on my pants and followed the boys to where their father was lying. Upon arriving at the home we found his father on the kitchen floor gasping for breath. Little did we know that he had experienced a massive heart attack. The medics arrived a short time later and administered CPR, but it was too late. He passed from this life a few hours later.

From that point, I decided to spend as much time as possible with the two boys because they needed a male role model since the rest of their family was in India. When I would play with my son Marcus, and daughter Chantal, in the back yard, I would include the two boys. I just recently received a phone call from Sasha after more than ten years of losing touch; He expressed his appreciation of my spending time with him and his brother during those years and after the death of his father. The lesson here is that you never know if some young person is watching you and the impact you can have on the lives of others.

My father taught me that winning is important but losing can be the better life lesson. We tend to learn from our failures significantly more than from our successes. If we always win, we sometime loose the hunger to get to the next level. His praise was as swift as his punishment and we are better off because of what we endured back then. In retrospect, we had two parents who loved us very much. Though we were not rich from an economic standpoint, we were blessed with a rich heritage and a solid family foundation. If there is a point where we need to refocus on family values, self respect and personal integrity, it's now.

Our family tree was made up of a list of characters any of who would have provided a writer with his or her life's work. There were names like Bo Bo, Tukufu, Ruby, Tutt, Jitter, Little Man, Skip, Mickey, Bay Bay, Bubba, Sweet, Sugar, Champ, Baby Sister, Little Sister, Doll and many others who made the war worth fighting. The most talented of writers could not have written a story equal to our adventures. It had indeed been an incredible journey from my grandparents Ed and Parthenia Dean's old farm house in Hope Hull, Ala., to places like Massachusetts, Ohio, California, Michigan, Georgia, Missouri, and many other places where the Dean Freeman migration has taken us. The war was now starting to heat up a bit. I was just beginning to learn just how the world viewed people of color and how that view would fuel my personal war within.

Chapter III

Bare Necessities

The greatest thing in the world is not so much where we stand as it is what direction we are moving.
                                            Oliver Wendell Holmes

Though we were somewhat sheltered from our poor socioeconomic status, we were taught to make good of what we had. Dad would make our kites from dried shag-weed limbs tied in the shape of a cross, covered carefully by pages from old newspapers and bound by paste made of flour and water. The tail was made of strips of cloth from old rags that were lying around. The string was pieced together from old package cord. If we were lucky, Dad would buy us a brand new ball of string from Mr. Tony's store. Back then, string sold for a whopping 6 cents. We would rap the string in a cross stitch around the control stick. This method was used to control the string release in high winds.

Approximately 300 to 400 yards from our back yard was an open field with hills of red dirt stacked as if they were mountains. We called the place the "DUMP". Who knew what was in those mounds of dirt. Our communities were used as dumping grounds for the waste and trash from the more affluent neighborhoods. The "dump" was a perfect setting for launching our home made kites. There were no trees or power lines to be concerned with. You could hear the wind whistling through those mounds of dirt like a tea-kettle on a red hot stove.

Our Dad was a master kite builder. The kites that he made were a notch above those found in the store. Kite building is a lost art now because everything is mass produced and of lesser quality. Our baseball games were made possible by a broom handle which represented the bat and tightly wrapped rags rolled into a round ball and secured with tape. During basketball games there were lots of "jaw jacking" and "talking smack" back in the day, but it was a matter of clean competition and friendly rivalry and never affected our friendship. Today on the playgrounds of our cities that same jaw jacking will get you killed. This new generation is an "in your face" generation which does not value life as we did. This hip hop generation lives for today with little future focus. I call them Boomerangers because they will throw themselves out into society without a plan. If their plan works, they are fine. If it doesn't, they return to live with their parents no matter their age.

Games like *Alabama Hit The Hammer*, *Jacks*, *Hide and Seek*, *Marbles*, *Doodley Bug*, and *Hop Scotch* have now been replaced by video games, soccer, tennis, golf, bowling and other sports that were either off limits or not available to us because they were reserved primarily for the upper class. We had a tendency to make our marks in football, basketball and track.

Back then walking along the Danky tracks, sliding down the coal covered hill that connected to our yard and catching tad poles out of the stream that ran between the houses, was what we considered fun. Kids today wouldn't be caught rolling an old tire for fun. When I show my kids pictures of us back then with our car tires, they laugh hysterically. They are so removed from those simple things that were special to us. There is an entitlement mentality in the current generation that just won't allow the majority to accept the simple life. Because we are more able to give to our kids more than we were given, we have contributed to their current state.

Though it seems strange behavior today, we would actually eat the red clay and chalky dirt that was in our yard. Actually, it didn't taste that bad. It was not that we didn't have food to eat but just that it was something to do and fun. Apples, oranges and candy were things that we received only on certain special days like holidays and birthdays. My kids find it hard to believe that when we were growing up, we sometimes only received a bag of fruit nuts and candy for Christmas and a pair of jeans if we were lucky. The occasional toy was a real treat. We sometimes wonder why our kids are spoiled; well consider this: we, as middle class parents, have brought them up in the land of milk and honey. Though we are not all experiencing our cut of the nation's pie, it seems OK to give our kids $130 Michael Jordan tennis shoes, $300 cell phones, $400 IPODS, $600 video games, and then we give all of these things without requiring them to do chores or have other household responsibilities. And we wonder why they are spoiled? Unfortunately, in homes where resources are limited, spending on these items tends to rival those in homes having significant resources.

Our elder population had a strong belief in God but that same belief made them quite vulnerable to the "tent" preachers and get rich scams of the era. The television evangelist got rich asking them to send in money for prayer cloths and other symbols of God's blessings. They were not interested in spreading God's word but instead, gaining wealth through deception. Even today many of our elderly people spend most of their hard earned money reaching for that elusive wish for wealth and happiness. Sometimes their life savings end up on the casino tables and slot machines in Las Vegas.

As a result of our not wanting our children to experience the hardships that we experienced, we fail to teach them how to get these things themselves and not feel an entitlement. We were required to cut the grass, mop the kitchen floor, take out the garbage, clean the bath room, wash the car, pull weeds out of the yard and flower beds, etc. You would think that we would transfer those same ideals to our children but we didn't. We are so afraid that they won't love us that we turn our heads to obvious learning situations. Our parents used "tough love" to teach us in a manner that it would serve us later. They knew how to say "no" when no surely was the best answer for us. They wanted our respect and didn't worry about whether their decision was popular or not.

Imagination played an important part of our world. It served to magnify our vision of not how things were but how things could be. Those were the dreams that were mentioned earlier. Hope seemed to be all we had to hold on to. While our white counterparts were learning and preparing for the new technological world, we did our best to just stay afloat with our inferior resources and lack of knowledge of the outside world. How could we be equal when we started so far behind? Our school facilities, our used books handed down through obsolescence from the white schools, our sports programs, our curriculum, our lunch programs, our school subsidy were all less than what the white kids had who we would eventually have to compete with for jobs.

Sure we grew up under the so called separate but equal doctrine but that was a joke. Everything was separate but nothing was equal. How can anyone consider separate eating facilities, separate water fountains, separate schools, separate rest rooms, sitting in the balcony at movies, sitting in the back of the bus, living in separate communities, as equal? It was definitely separate but there was nothing equal about it. The only times we even saw white folks were when the police drove through the neighborhood, or the ice cream man, insurance men, the guy driving the garbage truck, the cop hovering over the chain gang or on that rare occasion when Daddy or Mama would take us to town. We didn't fear white people, we just didn't know or understand them and they didn't understand or want to understand us. The white schools were not allowed to pay us in competitive sports, particularly football and basketball. They were considered superior and would not risk the idea of it not being true.

The idea of believing that it was true was much more powerful than finding out through participating in the competitive arena. Their scouts would frequently visit our games to assess our ability in case the races were forced to compete with each other. Their findings would not make it any easier for them to support integration. Many studies have been done on the genetic make up of the black athlete but I can tell them that there is no significant difference between white and black athletes other than desire. Many choose to believe that the black athlete had a different genetic make-up. They choose to believe that we were more like animals and built for speed and jumping ability and lacked the cognitive skills. That's why for many years blacks were not allowed to play positions like quarterback in football or become coaches in any sport outside the black community. It was a form of brainwashing which had as its purpose leading blacks away from strategic positions where cognitive planning and thinking was the core skill required. Sports were our focal point because of the inferior educational process. A person tends to excel in those things that he or she has as a focal point.

Plessey vs. Ferguson and Brown vs. the Board of Education were cases that brought the separate but equal ideology to the fore front of the news. The Plessey vs. Ferguson case established the "separate but equal" doctrine that pervaded life in the American South for over 50 years. The decision enabled the expansion of "separate but equal" to pervade many aspects of daily life for people in states throughout the South, where segregation became an institution. Schools, public facilities, restaurants, hotels, theaters, public transportation, etc. adopted the "separate but equal" policy to segregate African Americans away from whites and in most cases, make the best facilities inaccessible to us. Details of this case was obtained from the American History Profile.

The "separate but equal" doctrine was struck down, finally, in 1954 with the Brown vs. the Board of Education decision. The 1954 United States Supreme Court decision in *Oliver L. Brown et.al. v. the Board of Education of Topeka (KS)* is among the most significant judicial turning points in the development of our country. Originally led by Charles H. Houston, and later Thurgood Marshall and a formidable legal team, it dismantled the legal basis for racial segregation in schools and other public facilities. By declaring that the discriminatory nature of racial segregation . . . "violates the 14th amendment to the U.S. Constitution, which guarantees all citizens equal protection of the laws," **Brown v. Board of Education** laid the foundation for shaping future national and international policies regarding human rights. *Brown v. Board of Education* was not simply about children and education. The laws and policies struck down by this court decision were products of the human tendencies to prejudge, discriminate against, and stereotype other people by their ethnic, religious, physical, or cultural characteristics. Ending this behavior as a legal practice caused far reaching social and ideological implications, which continue to be felt throughout our country. The *Brown* decision inspired and galvanized human rights struggles across the country and around the world. (Brown Foundation *for Educational Equity, Excellence and Research*).

It would be very valuable to our youngsters today to revisit those Supreme Court ruling to see just how far we have come and yet how far we still have to go. Even with the election of the first black president in the history of this great country, there is still much to be done in human affairs, revamp of the socio economic system, and equal rights for all.

Chapter IV

The Early Years

The declaration of Independence is kind of a war song; A stately and passionate chant of human freedom.
—***Moses Ceit Tyler***

Our early years could be summed up very simply as poor, economically deprived but happy. Though we were not a part of the middle class, we had Mother and Daddy to make sure that we had clean clothes and food to eat. I was never a very good student though I had excellent teachers who made it seem as if I were. Hooper City School was where our education started. Mrs. Langford, my first grade teacher, had a heart that was as big as she was. It was her premise that if you were proficient at reading, writing, and arithmetic, you were well on the way to a solid foundation in just about any field you chose. It was definitely my misfortune to be born the youngest and to have to follow my sister and brother through the early grades. The teachers expected me to do as well as they did. Wrong! They were much better students than I was and I had to work twice as hard to keep up. To a degree, it was a blessing because it gave me the competitive drive to make it over the hurdles that were to come.

As I reflect back on those earlier years, most of our memorable accomplishments could be tracked to a much vaunted discipline, that of a solid school foundation and a loving stable home life. Dad would always find a way to make ends meet. There weren't any jobs too hard or too dirty for him to tackle and he did it with pride and dignity. Mother also did her part to support the family. Each morning she would make the long trip across the mountain to wash, clean and iron for the white folks.

Isn't it strange that our mothers cooked food, cleaned their homes, raised their children including breast feeding but were never respected enough to have a seat at their table. That was indicative of the Old South. Of course there were the occasional Christmas money and hand-me-down clothes but these could not make up for the sacrifices made by our black mothers and the dedication that they showed to their white employers. Though they were paid a small amount for their services, they were not given the respect that their hard work and dedication deserved. There were many white families who did not fit the old stereotype of administering raciest and unfair treatment toward their workers. Many of these families felt sympathetic to the plight of their maids but realized that there was little they could do because of the times.

Birmingham, Ala. was a large, small town. I mean, it was large in land mass, but small in social seeding. During the early sixties, there were hot beds of racial indifference and separatism in the city. A city guided by now renowned Governor George Wallace, better known for his standing in the door of the University of Alabama to prevent the integration of the institution by Autherine Lucy, its first black student. It became the center of national attention, not because of any great achievements, but instead because of its image as a window of injustice with clouded panes of racial hatred, bigotry and murder. George Wallace has departed this life but the separate BUT UNEQUAL attitudes still exist today in many of the corridors of towns and cities all over this country.

Imagine this city, with its pictorial setting and huge iron statue of a man standing on top of Red Mountain holding a flare which glows red when there had been a fatal accident and green when the city had been accident free. Let your mind imagine the dusty winds that brought the many smells of cotton gins, steel and iron ore factories, freshly baked bread, red clay, chicken factories, and the smog hanging like a colorful quilt over the city. For those not familiar with quilts, they were made from pieces of cloth sewed together in numerous patterns and each section was stuffed with cotton to increase the comfort level. Many of these quilts were colorful and well constructed to handle the wear and tear of use over the years. If we could have been just like those old quilts, bounded together to make each of us that much stronger, our elders who have gone on to eternity would have an everlasting smile on their faces. The smell of cotton gins and iron ore factories and the separate water fountains and facilities had a major impact on our beliefs, our culture and everyday lives from the southern black prospective.

The little three-room double tenant house that we lived in was a picture to be painted. The place did have character! The structure was made of old gray plank boards arranged in an overlapping manner so that the rain water could not get to the foundation, a series of brick supports which were placed in periodic locations to support its foundation. There was a 10-foot opening at the back of the house from the porch to the ground which served us well as a place to play on rainy days. To the front of the structure, the ground gradually elevated and the space gave way to packed clay and rock.

The clearing at the front of the house was less than two feet while the back had at least 10 feet of clearance from ground to structure. In the far right rear of the house was an old wash tub used for washing clothes and taking the infamous Saturday baths. Mama spent many hours scrubbing clothes in that same old tin tub using the rubbing board to get the clothes clean. I remember that sometimes during our baths in that old tub, we would talk to Mama through a hole in the kitchen floor. Those floors may have had a few holes here and there but man were they sturdy. The wood used in those days seemed more pliable than the wood is today. It didn't seem to warp or rot as easily. On the back porch were our wash pan and an old Kenmore washing machine which my father was finally able to purchase for mother to keep her off her knees washing clothes in that old tin tub. I must tell you that as a young inquisitive boy, I was intrigued by the wringer on the machine and how cool it was that it was able to squeeze the water out of the clothes which Mama had usually done by hand. This one particular day my curiosity got the best of me and I decided to feed the next piece of clothing through the rollers.

Well, you can just about imagine what happened next. As I fed the shirt through the roller, I was distracted by Bill who had called from the yard for me to come down and play. I held on to the shirt too long and my fingers on my left hand were pulled through the roller. Hearing my shrill and high pitch screams, my sister Liz quickly showed up on the back porch. Boy was I glad to see her. She was often asked to keep and eye on me and had a sense of mind to disconnect the washer by pulling the power cord out of the wall socket. By that time, my hand was through the roller. I was more concerned by what mother would do and less about the condition of my arm. Luck was indeed on my side and the rollers had enough "play" in them that my hand and arm were not crushed. In fact, it was also very beneficial that I was so young and my bones were more like, as mom would say, gristles and would bend but not break. Boy was I glad that she was right.

As we continue to visualize the old home place, these words help us to understand the importance of this period. In the rear corner stood a storage shed for accumulating coal and wood for cooking and heating. Our major coal and wood supply came from the "Danky" that passed our house on its way to the drop off point in a little town called Seraton which was further down the tracks. The Danky was a funny looking train appearing as if it were coming and going at the same time. It was used to haul coal and wood to points on the transit line. In route, the coal and wood would sometimes fall off the train, down an embankment and into our yard. There were times when the coal and wood in the shed became very low and Dad would climb on the back cars of the Danky to give the wood and coal a little assistance in falling. Some of you may say that he was stealing the wood and coal. Much of that wood and coal would fall off the train anyway because the cars were overloaded so dad would rather we have it than have it fall along the track where it would not be used. Dad did what it took to provide for his family and did it within the framework of the law.

There were approximately 18 steps leading to our back porch. Many nights on those steps the neighborhood gang gathered to play games and tell tales. We played such games as Alabama Hit the Hammer and Hide and Seek. You may think that the game Alabama Hit the Hammer High or Low had something to do with Alabama but it didn't. It was simply a game that we played that required you to start on the top step of the back stairway and the first one who guessed the correct hand that the rock was in, got to move further down the steps. One of the older children would always be the leader and controlled the process including holding the stone in one hand or the other. One hand held high, the other hand held low and each individual would chose either the high hand or the low one. The first one to select the hand with the stone in it with the most consistency and get to the bottom step was the winner. As you can see, we lived quite a simple life without the complications and pressures that kids place on themselves today. Though we didn't have much, we were happy.

The older kids would tell ghost stories to scare the younger ones. These stories usually included graveyards, ghost or "haints" as we called them. Walking through graveyards, as we often had to do to get to certain parts of the community, was a scary thing when you are young. Though we didn't realize that dead people can't hurt anyone, they can make you hurt yourself from the fear factor. In the back yard was that larger than life tree that you were introduced to earlier on this trip. A stream with minnows, tadpoles, crayfish, and plenty of green slime and the dirtiest water you ever wanted to see, ran through the center of the back yard. The ditch was the line of demarcation between the properties. Off center and to the left of the yard was the "out house". The out house was our toilet which was, as the name implies, the house outside. On the back porch was an old wash basin that we were required to use to wash our hands and faces before meals and at bed time. That old porch made strange noises when you walked across it but it was sturdy. Wood seemed stronger in those old houses for some reason.

Of course we were not the only family using that yard. The house was double tenant which required the two families to share the facilities. Our neighbors were Mr. Fred and Mrs. Suzie Arbe. Their daughter's names were Dott and Beth, both of whom were nice in a strange sort of way. We never knew whether the two had jobs or not because one or the other was always around the house. They both were in their 20's and seemed quite distant from their parents. Employment for young women who had no formal education was limited to working as clerks in stores, or serving as maids. They seemed to spend most of their time washing and cleaning for Mr. Fred and Mrs. Suzie. Mr. Fred would often come home with a snout full and would feel bad afterwards for letting us kids see him that way. He was really a good person who suffered from the lack of self-worth and accomplishment. He wanted so badly to be, as he would say; a "somebody." What he failed to realize was that he was a somebody; He was a somebody who was becoming a nobody at the bottom of a bottle.

On the other side of the line of demarcation (the stream), was a little red shingled house occupied on one side by the good Rev. Gray, the community "jack leg" preacher and the family of my best friend Richard Allred Kemp. For those not familiar with the term "jack legged" preacher, it refers to one who was a preacher without a church and would quote from the bible to the kids in the neighborhood. Though he was older than life itself, it was not hard for us kids to identify with him because he was our conscience, who we really were as a people. He was a combination of preacher, teacher, doctor, lawyer and philosopher.

Across the large open field, south of our house, was another line of shotgun houses. These were the homes of the older members of our neighborhood group, Junior and Patricia Campbell and Arthur Taylor, better known to the kids as Bee. To the front of our house was Mr. Tony's grocery store and juke joint, as clubs were called in those days. Mr. Tony was a nice white man who would let everyone in the community have groceries on credit until pay day. Back then, the trust factor was much stronger than today and people paid their obligations. Behind his store lived one of the strangest but most interesting old ladies by the name of Ms Lucky. Unlike Mr. Tony, she seemed to hate children and designed her yard to keep us out. The fence around her yard was made of chicken wire, barbed wire, broken glass, plywood sections and numerous other hazards. She was deadly serious about her right to privacy and believe me, we respected her wishes.

In this little community of Hooper City, tucked quietly in the mountain shadows of Birmingham, we were somewhat shielded from the overt and covert acts of racism around us. It wasn't that often that we left the community at all. We were one of only a handful of people who were fortunate enough to have a car. It was not fashionable for blacks and whites to socialize during that time period. Whites owned all the businesses with the exception of a few Mom and Pop stores and barber shops. Most of the black families were subjected to second class citizenship which meant poor or no services. The water fountains and restrooms were separate and labeled by race. We were called "colored" back then and it was not until much later in our development as a people that we became "Negroes". The term "Black" came many, many years later.

In the history of this great country, there has been no other race of people who have had to struggle so hard for their identity as those of us of African decent. No other race of people was required to have a voter's rights act legislated to merely exercise their right to vote. Through this dilemma, we have been taught to set our goals as high as the moon so that if we fall short we would still land among the stars. We were taught to be strong and to accept responsibility for our actions. Through all of the prejudice, discrimination and hatred, we were taught to love, forgive and respect all individuals. Our forefathers seemed to hold on to the belief that love would, in the end, conquer all. Even though it was something to look forward to, it seemed out of reach in my time here on earth. The hill still today seems too steep to climb.

Chapter V

Character Builders

Ethics and equity and the principles of justice do not change with the calendar.

—David Lawrence

It is so incredible how the mind has the ability to store some vivid memory of times gone by while other parts of our past have been depressed so deeply and not easily retrieved. The memories that remain are what I call character builders. They are the heart and soul of our psychological development, the straw that stirs our drink. I can remember so vividly the mornings at the kitchen table, the smell of mama's grits, eggs, and home made biscuits and the self ground A&P coffee perking in the little silver pot on top of the old Kenmore stove used not just for cooking but to help the old pot bellied heater in the middle room heat the house during the bitterly cold winters.

We had often wondered why Mama never would sit down to eat with us. She would wait until we had finished before taking even a bite of food. It was much later as adults that we finally realized that there really wasn't enough food to feed us all. She would let us eat first and would eat what was left, if she ate at all. Mother would make every sacrifice to see that we had the bare necessities. Mama was always the last to bed and the first to rise. Daddy always got up early to go to work and Mama would have his clothes and lunch box ready. It became the tradition that daddy would save a portion of one of his sandwiches to give to our dog Tiger who always met the car when daddy got off from work to get his Scooby snack.

On those blustery winter nights the three of us would huddle closely together in that old oak bed with only a thin layer of cover between us and the thin chilly night air. There were many times that we would wake to find Mama laying on top of us to keep us warm because blankets were only a mild preventative from the bitter cold nights. Now that's what I call real love. When it was time for us to get up for school, Mom would have already filled the pot bellied stove with coal and wood until it turned red from the heat. The place was warm and cozy and breakfast was on the table. That was an era where it was customary for families to sit together during main meals. It was required. Today, everyone is in the buffet mode. We grab a plate, fill it with food and go off to our respective private places. That, in itself, is an indication of how the basic fabric of the family has been torn apart.

Many kids were not fortunate enough to have both parents still in the home as ours were. Dad worked many jobs from the railroad to trucking lines. He was not one to let anyone get too close to him, not even our mother to a degree. He seemed so cold and distant at times. Dad was a strict disciplinarian in his own way. How I do remember those loud and seemingly endless whippings. Mama would scold, whip and love you at the same time. The punishment seemed to hurt her more than it did us. Now Dad was a totally different story. He would whip and talk at the same time while biting on his tongue. When he was finished he would not say another word to you and you knew to keep your distance.

The thing that hurt most about the whippings was more often than not, we had to go out into the field and bring back the switch to be used in our own flogging. That's right, I said flogging because those beatings went beyond whipping. Mama would say, "go and get me a switch because I am going to tear you up", and that she did. The switch had to be strong and sturdy and it had to be green so that it would not break. There is something intimidating about having to cut the switch that was to be used in your punishment. The word "switch" was a feared word in the household. When the whipping did start, the whistling sound of the switch could be heard for blocks.

If Dad didn't want to wait for us to get a switch, he would use the razor strap. Now, those of you who know what I am talking about know that there is no other whipping, like a razor strap whipping. A razor strap is the thing used by barbers to sharpen their razors prior to giving a customer a shave. It is long, wide and made of that good leather that won't break under any condition. Today, those whippings would be called "child abuse". If the whippings that we got were considered child abuse, as they sometimes are today, our parents would have been given life in prison. They truly believed that if you spared the rod, you would spoil the child. Guess what, in spite of those whippings, we turned out OK. Maybe if those were still allowed, we wouldn't be experiencing the rash of violence that is all around us today.

We were taught to judge people not by color or race but by their individual merit and behavior. We were all made better by that type of "tough love" that they believed in. Our folks were always the religious type taking us to church and instilling the values in us needed to have both spiritual and physical growth. Mama was Baptist and Daddy was Methodist. I never quite understood why there were different religions because there was only one God. We were more accustomed to Baptist and would always go to church with Mama. Our early development was based on our parent's "Ten Commandments" and their requiring that we learn to accept responsibility for our actions. Do unto others as we would have them do to us. If you get knocked down, don't just lay there, get up and brush yourself off and go at it one more time. It's not what happens to you that count, it's what happens in you that matters, as the old saying goes.

These were the commandments that were to shape our lives. These commandments were strictly enforced and punishment was swift and painful when violated.

- Treat others as you would like to be treated
- Good and bad people come in all colors
- Create your own opportunities through hard work
- Love God first, then each other
- Success comes before work only in the dictionary
- Honor and respect the elders, they are our foundation
- Always tell the truth no matter how much it hurts. It saves a lot of pain later (that part was really hard)
- You are limited only by your personal desires
- To get respect, you must give it
- Don't make the same mistake twice

I don't have to tell you how difficult it was living to those commandments when it was so cool to "do your own thing". Doing your own thing in our house could be dangerous to ones health. I can hear the old man saying, "What are you doing boy, you smelling yourself. Boy, I brought you into this world and, by God, I will take you out of it."

Today, I constantly remind my children of these things:

- Listen to those wise older trail blazers, they know about places you still have to go
- Respect all women, they are the foundations of the families
- Stay away from drugs and keep your future
- Never give up because success is just over the horizon

- Remember and learn from the past to enrich the future
- Use time wisely . . . for it's but a few minutes
- Focus on who you are and not who others want you to be. A goal that is too easily accomplished may have been set to low
- Behavior, attitude, and aptitude, will affect altitude
- Take care of your health . . . . once gone, it's hard to get it back

When the old folks said that the devil was going to get you, you may as well pack your bags and sit out on the porch and wait because the sucker surely would be coming. Back in those days, children respected what the older people would say. Today, not only do some young people not respect the senior generation, they do not respect themselves. Gang warfare, drugs, easy money, disrespectful lyrics in songs, wearing pants half way down their hips, tattoos, talking back to parents, loud music, and video mania is the backdrop of the new generation. There are many in this generation that are on the right track and has taken the correct fork in the road. They are the ones that I would hope that the media will focus on to hopefully assist in motivating the others. This generation, as a whole has the technology at their disposal, a greater competency in cyber space, and a tremendous amount of peer pressure. Those able to negotiate these difficult waters will be the victors.

I remember the time when while playing in the back yard, I saw the prettiest red bird this side of creation. It was sitting about thirty feet from where I was standing. As most kids do, my first thought was to pick up a rock because we all thought we had the title of master rock thrower. We usually didn't come close to hitting anything particularly a bird that would constantly move. I slowly bent down to find the perfect saucer rock like the one we used to water skip (sliding thin rocks over the surface of the water).

As I stood to throw, knowing that I had but one chance in a million and not really thinking about hitting anything, the little bird seem to freeze as the rock drew near. I'd thrown the rock with considerable force with the expectation that, as in the past, the pretty little bird would just flutter away. As the stone drew closer, something told me that this time was different, the little bird just stood there panic stricken. I covered my eyes as the rock first struck the ground and then heard a soft thud sound. I immediately knew that I had realized my worst fear, that I had actually hit the target. I really didn't mean it but the damage was done. The rock hit the bird directly behind the neck killing it instantly. That bright Sunday morning seemed to instantly turn to gloom. Dark clouds seemed to cover the sky, the wind started to blow harder and harder as the little dust tornadoes encircled me. I was expecting the devil himself to appear at any moment because Mama had often told us that the devil would get us if we did bad things. Mama made me pick the bird up and bury it in the yard and then to ask God to forgive me for what I had done. It took me a long time to get over that day. I have to say that being a boy, I still continued to throw at the birds but never again did I hit the target.

Chapter VI

The Middle Years

Some men see things as they are and say why? I see things as they never were, and ask why not?
—George Bernard Shaw

The mid 50s and 60s were times of continued racial indifference and dramatic change. Victor Hugo had said, "Nothing, neither an army nor a legislature nor even an armed law officer can withstand the strength of an idea whose time has come." This was a time when an idea and a people's political time had arrived, according to millions of black voters.

Though the Emancipation Proclamation and the north's victory in the civil war ended slavery, southern whites were determined to keep their former slaves in their control. In the reconstruction period (1867-1877), the tide was turned briefly by Congress. Blacks got to vote and former slaves were elected and became a part of the Washington elite. But as it had done in the past, the old order crept back. It was hard letting go of the past. A whole structure of racial degradation was hammered into place. Poll taxes thwarted the black vote and Jim Crow laws made humiliation a daily fact of life. Thuggary and murder by the Klan choked off progress. Even the

Supreme Court assisted in the institutional racism by maintaining, for more than 58 years the doctrine of separate but equal. Blacks moved north in numbers seeking the good life and to get away from the Jim Crow laws of the south. They found themselves living in worse conditions than they'd left behind and even farther from the dream. In 1954, when segregation was ruled unconstitutional, the true fight for equality and justice was launched.

When Rosa Parks said her firm and profoundly significant "no" to taking a back seat on the bus, it ignited the long awaited initiative and show of solidarity. It was December 1, 1955, when she refused to give up her seat to a white bus rider. Throughout the south such degrading discrimination was common practice and within the law. When she did not give in, she was arrested and charged with violating a city ordinance. Her bravery started an explosion of pride in the black community and united more than 40,000 blacks of Montgomery (Population 121,000 in 1955) in a successful resistance that eventually raised the awareness of a nation. A boycott of the city buses was organized by the NAACP. The boycott ended when the Supreme Court upheld a lower court ruling that segregation on buses was unconstitutional. This was also the beginning of the non-violent movement led by Dr. Martin Luther King, Jr. He was such a powerful leader that he even received concerns and criticism from other black leaders of that era.

Though Hooper City played an important part in my life and was significant in my early development, it was time to move on. Early on this particular morning, Dad took us on one of the family wish trips. We would often go around to some of the better neighborhoods and look at the beautiful homes. Little did we know that this particular trip would mark the beginning of another chapter in my war within. We had been riding for several hours when we came upon a very nice community called Titusville. There were but a few homes completed in this obviously new community, but boy were they special.

As our green 1951 Chevrolet rounded a curve in what was call Honey Suckle Circle, Dad pointed to a large green house on the left, "How do you like that one," he said to Mama. Mama just shook her head as if to say "dream on". "I would daddy," I spouted out. Dad just smiled and immediately turned the Chevy into the graveled drive of that beautiful house. We just stared at the place for, it seemed, a long time when Dad got out and walked a few steps in front of the car. He stopped and motioned for us to follow. "We are going to get into trouble," I said to Mama. I was sure that these beautiful homes were owned by white folks and they would not be happy if they knew that we not only was looking at their house but that we had the gall to park in their driveway. Mama just shook her head and started to get out. After all, we were not supposed to be there.

As we walked the length of the house on the gravel drive, the echo from our shoes could be heard for miles it seemed. At that point, there were only a few of the nice houses completed. Others were being built and around them were, it seemed, miles of open field and rag weed. Dad seemed quite at ease for some reason and again surprised us by saying, "Let's see what it looks like inside." Now I knew that he had lost his cotton picking mind by going into other people's home. Dad reached into his pocket and pulled out a key to open the door. The house had more space and rooms that I had ever seen. It had a living room a dinning room, kitchen, den or TV room, and to top it off they had brought the "out house" inside. After a few trips around the inside of that dream home, it was time to go. Back to reality, back to Hooper City, the dream was coming to an end.

As our car slowly pulled away from the house, Dad asked, "How would we like to live there?" Mama responded with "maybe one day we will be able to afford something like that. At lease it gives us something to dream about." At that point, dad gave the keys to Mama and said, "Be careful what you wish for because that day has come and dreams do sometimes come true." Mama was visibly stunned. She was speechless and the tears started to flow. She had often prayed that we would someday move to better surroundings, a better neighborhood, a better life. This was indeed another chapter in our lives and a new beginning, but what we didn't know was that racism was alive and well, even in such a wonderful spot.

As other families moved into that peaceful community, a feeling of belonging and security was evident. Though I really did miss the old double tenant house and my special friends, it was time to move on. There were new friends: Alfred, Edward, Ronnie, Junior, Ricky, Don, Chubby, Carol, Lois, Tyrone, Herman, Faye, Jan, Butch, and many others. This was the beginning of a period of false hope, a hope that was to be dampened by blatant racism. There was hope of a more peaceful world, faith that God would lead us out of the racist past. But there was still a hidden fear that things had not changed but had moved across town.

As I look back on that community and the many fine people that have cancer now and others who have gone on to be with God, I wonder why there were so many cancer deaths in that one place, Mrs. and Mr. Belcher, Mrs. and Mr. Owens, Mrs. and Mr. Dyodell, Mr. and Mrs. Hunter, Mr. and Mrs. Houser, Mr. and Mrs. Harris, Mr. And Mrs. Zeigler, Mrs. Jordan. During that time many of the black communities were built on land that, at one time, was the city dumping grounds. Radon gas and other by products of the land and dumping could have been the cause of the many cancer deaths in that community. It is possible that we will never know the REAL truth of extensive numbers of cancer deaths in that great little community.

These were still difficult days. Days that brought bombing of neighborhood churches, death of innocent citizens, demonstrations for the rights that should have been guaranteed by the constitution, attacks by vicious police dogs, and the use of fire hoses on innocent demonstrators. Racism had proven to be a formative foe whose breed had been kept alive in the dark corridors of hate brought on by groups like the John Birch Society, the Klan, and the government. In that city that was sometimes called "bombingham" instead of Birmingham, King's Southern Christian Leadership Conference (SCLC) intensified the pressure and tension by demonstrating against the atrocities of the time. Many were jailed and treated inhumanely. I have never forgotten the day that we received word that my sister Liz had been arrested for demonstrating in downtown Birmingham. She was a member of the SCLC movement and one of King's close consultants. Many of the demonstrators were placed in holding cells made of barbed wire located on the outside of the Police Department. The demonstrators were subjected to demeaning insults as well as being subjected to the elements.

Just after the highly successful march on Washington and King's famous "I have a dream" speech, four little black school girls were killed when a bomb exploded as they attended church at the Sixteenth Street Baptist Church in downtown Birmingham. One of the girls was the daughter of my teacher, Mrs. McNair. Her name was Denise McNair, a beautiful and gifted young lady with a bright future who never got the opportunity to share in the dream, to showcase her talents, to make a difference. Her death was not in vain. Many like Denise gave their lives for the cause, for the dream. It would have been so easy to hate those who were responsible but our parents taught us to pray for those who seek to hurt you and seek to forgive as the bible teaches. Believe me, back then I found that pretty hard, and I still do. No one, has the right to take another life. God gave it and only God should take it away. Those responsible for the bombings saw themselves as protectors for a way of life which time had passed. These events were just a few of many that were to take place in our communities by these cowards. Nights were time to worry and hope that the darkness would not bring more tragedy. Under the cover of night, white hate groups would come with their home made bombs and blasting caps with an aim to destroy blacks who stood in their way. They would first plant a decoy bomb with a timer set to explode in the early morning hours, just as most were getting up for morning breakfast.

The initial bomb had as its purpose to draw people from their homes because of their curiosity. As individuals would gather around the location of the first bomb, a carefully planned second explosion would occur approximately ten to fifteen minutes after the first. It consisted of a large amount of explosive, metals and other piercing objects used to kill or injure. Those incidents are indicative of the gap that was ever so present between the races. Not only were we not liked and appreciated by other races, we sometimes didn't treat each other with the respect and dignity that we were so desperately seeking.

I remember a time when I returned to the old community to celebrate my high school reunion. The guys that didn't like me then still didn't like me and didn't remember why. After all those years, they couldn't remember why they didn't, but they were convinced that they didn't. As it is with hate, it eats away at the fabric of a society primarily without reason. Hate not only destroys the hated, it destroys the hater. That didn't seem to matter in the Old South. All that mattered was that the races were to remain separate and there was to be no mixing under any circumstances.

Chapter VII

Later Years

You will become as small as your controlling desires, as great as your dominant aspiration.
—James Allen

My high school years were both boring, eventful, and life altering to say the least. Sports became a means to an end for many black students including me. Sports were not only a way to display our God given talent but also a way out of the ghetto dogma that had many black men enslaved and hopeless. I remember vividly, the long walks up Six Avenue to Ullman High School. There would be hundreds of students making that long walk not only to school but also back home because we had no school buses. We would see the school buses from the white schools passing us by as they headed to a different part of town. That was the period that ushered in busing to integrate the school systems.

Though public schools were technically desegregated in 1954 by the U.S. Supreme Court decision in *Brown vs Board of Education*, many were still *de facto* segregated due to inequality in housing and racial segregation in neighborhoods. In the 1971 *Swann v. Charlotte-Mecklenburg Board of Education* ruling, the Supreme

Court allowed *Charlotte, North Carolina* and other cities nationwide to use mandatory busing and student assignment based on race to attempt to further integrate schools. However, in 1974's *Milliken v. Bradley* they placed an important limitation on *Swann* when they ruled that students could only be bused across district lines when evidence of *de jure* segregation across multiple school districts existed. (Source: Wikipedia, free encyclopedia)

In the 1970s and 1980s, under federal court supervision, many school districts implemented mandatory busing plans within their district. A few of these plans are still in use today. However, since the 1980s desegregation busing has been in decline. Even though school districts provided free *bus* transportation to and from students' assigned schools, those schools were in some cases many miles away from students' homes, which often presented problems to them and their families. In addition, many families were angry about having to send their children miles to another school in an unfamiliar neighborhood when there was an available school a short distance away. *White flight* reduced the effectiveness of busing, as large numbers of white families moved to suburban districts where their children would not be bused into increasingly black cities. Many whites who stayed moved their children into *private* or *parochial schools*; these effects combined to make urban school districts heavily black, reducing any effectiveness mandatory busing may have had. In addition, school districts started using *magnet schools*, new school construction, and more detailed computer-generated information to refine their school assignment plans.

Due to these efforts and the fact that housing patterns had changed, by the early 1990s, most school districts had been released from court supervision and ceased using mandatory busing to try to desegregate schools. However, many continued to provide school bus services because families had become accustomed to it. Those that didn't want busing to work, both white and black, claim that children were being bused to schools in dangerous neighborhoods, compromising their education and personal safety. The increased average distance of students from their schools also contributed to the reduced ability of students to participate in extracurricular activities and parents to volunteer for school functions although parent volunteering percentages were historically low in city schools. (Wikipedia)

The increased journey times to and from school—sometimes hours a day on buses—results in less time for recreation, study and (in the case of older students) employment and operating the buses costs a lot of money which would be better spent elsewhere in the education system. Radical busing plans could place enormous stresses on students and their parents—i.e., the transporting of children to very distant neighborhoods, the last-minute transfer of high school seniors who would not be able to graduate with their class and the sometimes annual redrawing of school district lines to attain racial balance. It was believed that these stresses led white middle-class families in many communities to desert the public schools and create a network of private schools.

Busing is claimed to have accelerated a trend of middle-class relocation to the suburbs of metropolitan areas. Both white and black parents who opposed forced busing claimed the existence of "white flight" based on the court decisions to integrate schools. Some parents claim that busing created even more tension for both economic and racial segregation, forcing cities to divide themselves along racial lines. They contend that the "white flight" to the suburbs has permanently eroded the tax base of major metropolitan areas, impairing the metropolitan areas' abilities to offer programs aimed at improving the plight of the minorities whom busing was allegedly supposed to benefit. It is also said that busing eroded the community pride and support that neighborhoods had for their local schools.

Baseball, football, and track taught us to be disciplined, yet creative, aggressive yet controlled, dependent on each other yet independent. Those years brought about a sense of identity not only because of the racial incidents of that time but because "Black Is Beautiful" became our battle cry. No longer were we ashamed of our black skin, no longer did we feel like second class citizens, and no longer did we have the old feeling of hopelessness. We were at the front lines of our war within.

Most of the older kids had started to leave the neighborhood in search of their futures. They were destined for colleges and jobs in other parts of the country. Many of us did not venture outside of Birmingham during the early years. Our only contact with the outside world was through reading. Our parents were not able to afford us the exposure to cultural events or educational opportunities consistent with our white counterparts. Having exposure to other parts of the country as well as other cultures would have added to the psychological and educational development so important in competing at higher levels of learning. My sister Liz had started to school at Miles College, a small school in the city of Fairfield, Alabama. My brother Bill had gone off to join Uncle Sam's Army in Ft. Hood Texas. I was, for the first time, home alone without the companionship of my siblings which added considerably to my "war within". I was not able to have the experiences that the kid in the movie *Home Alone* had. My parents kept close tabs on me at all times.

Things were not changing fast enough for me. My Mother called me restless and unsettled. She knew that I was wrestling with the "war" that was beginning to burn within me. She assured me that things would get better as long as we trusted in the Lord. I did believe in God but it was always my belief that God also expected us to put forth a degree of effort to make things change for ourselves. Now matter how the media tried to make us think that things and times were getting better, in my eyes they were remaining the same old stuff. Discrimination was very much blatant and quite openly practiced by those who wanted the past to be the menu for the future. George Wallace was making history by standing in the doorway of the University of Alabama as a gesture of the state's desire to keep "the good old days "alive and well" and to keep the first black student, Autherine Lucy, from breaking the color barrier at that prestigious school. There were difficult days ahead on both sides of the race card. Though separate facilities had been declared unlawful, there were still pockets of resistance making it clear that laws could be legislated but compassion and respect could not.

Our generation was one of very little patience for and tolerance of the events that had shaped the lives of those who had come before us. We were indeed "dreamers" of things that could be, not things that were. We knew from history that advancement on any front was always preceded by demonstrations and tremendous struggle. The demonstrations were to continue through the sixties and seventies. Jim Crow laws, dogs, fire hoses, and jail cells were to be the methods of awakening the conscience of a nation. The word "Jim Crow" was believed to be coined back in 1828 by a white entertainer named Thomas "Daddy" Rice who performed a minstrel act including a song called "Jump Jim Crow" in burned-cork black face and hobo rags, according to Douglas Brinkley in his novel "Rosa Park". Black face was used by white actors to mimic black folks.

Black men, more than ever, were being seen as a threat to the survival of the Old Southern attitudes. We had no status, few meaningful jobs, less education, yet we were considered some sort of a threat. You figure that one out because I can't. Attempts were being made to demoralize the will of our father, and brothers by employment tactics elevating our mothers and sisters to positions normally held by black men. More and more black men were taking up with white women, considered the forbidden fruit and causing even more tension between the races. For the first time, black men and women were starting to realize the impact of education on the future of our race. More black students were enrolling in predominately white institutions. The shackles that were binding us were beginning to give a bit. The private wars within each of us were just beginning to reach a boiling point.

Chapter VIII

Considering the Army

Progress is the sum of small victories won by individual human beings

—Catton

Before I venture into another most difficult time in my life, I would just like to share some data with you that will set the stage for my experience in the military. At this time in my life, there was a certain restless spirit that was tugging at me. I was faced with either college or the streets. The military was the farthest thing from my mind. During my trips to downtown Birmingham, I would see the signs with this big white man with a beard and a red white and blue hat on. The sign always said Uncle Sam Wants you! What did that mean? Over the years I was told that this was the invitation to join the military. Though I still had no intention of joining the military, I had started to give some thought to the possibility.

Vietnam, Iraq, the Persian Gulf, and the streets of our inner cities have claimed a generation of black men. In addition to these events are the added pressures of decreasing enrollment in colleges and universities, unemployment which affects the black male two fold over other groups, incarceration which claims more of our resources than does college, health care, lack of housing, stereotyping, and self destruction through homicides and drugs; all played a major role in the current plight of the black male.

According to the Schott Foundation for Public Education, most black men in the United States don't graduate from high school and only 35 percent of black male students graduate from high school in large cities like Chicago and only 26 percent in New York City. It is reported that young black male students have the lowest test scores, worst grades, highest drop-out rate, and worst behavior of all the students in the country. It is also becoming a disturbing trend that even if and when a young black male graduates from college in the U.S., there is a great chance that he is from Africa, the Caribbean, or Europe. The point that disturbs me as an American born black man is what is it about the drive and dedication of our young brothers here that seems different from those coming from other areas of the world. As a black American who has succeeded in the system, my opinion is that many of our young black men did not have the strong role models as we were growing up. Because it took both parents to make ends meet in many of our black families, boys were less likely to study, do homework and focus on the education process. Black families were more prone to divorce and absentee fathers forced mothers into the difficult task of raising a black male child. Please understand that this is one man's opinion and does not necessarily represent the feelings of others.

College is a privilege and a means to an end for most of us. We can no longer be satisfied with a high school education. Even with an undergraduate degree, your choices of careers are becoming limited. As more of our blue collar jobs are moved to lower labor and lower tax based countries, many of the remaining positions are requiring advanced degrees. In addition to that fact, many degreed people are flooding the market and competing for the fewer and fewer remaining jobs in a more service based market.

I am really tired of hearing the jokes such as if you want to hide something from a black man, place it in a book. As parents, particularly, of black males, we must emphasize the importance of reading, navigating the English language, mastering mathematical skills and learning multi languages. In my mind, those are just a few of the keys that will clean up the negative image that we black men have had to endure for so many years.

The prisons of this country have unfortunately become the playground for many of our young black resources. In fact, more than one million of our young resources are pumping iron and pressing license plates in our prisons today; These statistics exceed those of the rest of the world. According to the same report, this criminalization of our young men starts as early as elementary school with children as young as six and seven years of age being arrested in staggering numbers. Consider this, the schools that are preparing our young men teach them skills that will not make them competitive in this growing global economy.

The teachers that at one time had pride in growing our children are in record numbers choosing to jump a dying educational ship and take other professions or retire. The dilemma is made even more difficult because white teachers particularly in the southern states, are leaving black schools in record numbers. According to USA Report, Patrik Jonsson, January 21, 2003 edition, this is seen as a new form of segregation Certain neighborhoods in the South are weathering a new version of an old phenomenon: white flight. Across the region, white, often middle-class, Teachers are leaving schools dominated by African-Americans almost as fast as they arrive. Many are moving to schools districts with smaller populations of blacks, new studies show.

Critics see the exodus as a new form of segregation, encouraged by court rulings that no longer enforce racial diversity. But teachers say that cultural and economic barriers, not racial ones, are fueling the trend in a region where more than 40 percent of the public school population is black. At the very least, the growing shortage of white educators is creating a dilemma for black schools from Picayune County, Miss., to Decatur, Ga. Right now, there aren't enough black teachers to go around, either. "All the stars are aligned for white teachers to leave," says Gary Orfield, an education professor at Harvard University in Cambridge, Mass. "It's a combination of poverty and racial segregation, added to cultural differences, that all makes it tough for suburban teachers to figure out the black and Latino cultures."

In Georgia, the trend is as pronounced as anywhere: A new study from Georgia State University (GSU) in Atlanta says that 32 percent of white elementary school teachers left their posts at predominantly black schools in 2001—up from 18 percent in 1995. Moreover, they left well-to-do black districts at about the same rate as poorer ones. Recent studies in Texas, California, and North Carolina reach the same conclusion. The effect, critics say, is that black students aren't getting an equal shot at good schooling. The reason: As white teachers leave, many blacks are fleeing the profession, too, leaving a dearth of qualified teachers of any kind. "As a result, we have lots of classes being taught by substitute teachers, who don't usually have degrees and aren't licensed to teach anything," says Tom Clark, a former superintendent of the Picayune County, Miss., schools.

Other factors are contributing to the exodus. A recent schools building boom in Georgia created more job options for teachers—many of whom wanted to work closer to their own neighborhoods. What's more, many qualified teachers tend to leave lower-performing schools at faster rates.

But the authors of a new Harvard study on the "re-segregation" of the South believe the flight is rooted in something more ominous. They see it as an inevitable result of a backsliding society where white and black students increasingly go to different schools. They trace that divide, in part, to recent federal court decisions outlawing civil rights-era protections, such as busing and affirmative action in college admissions. What's more, fewer and fewer Southern schools are under court order to end discrimination.

As diversity diminishes, the problems become much more of a focus. Mr. Orfield notes that white teachers who grew up in integrated schools have less trouble adjusting to crowded hallways where most of the kids are black. Even practical complaints can mask deeper motivations. "It's race, not test scores, not income, that's the motivating factor, says David Sjoquist, a professor involved with the GSU study. "If there's a concern about safety simply because there are black people in the neighborhood, sociologists would say that's a form of racism."

Still, not everyone agrees that faulty motives are behind many of the white Teachers' decisions to leave. In many cases, it's more a matter of general frustration and unhappiness. "I don't think that the majority of these teachers who leave are racist," says Mike Worthington, the white principal of predominantly black Avondale High School in suburban Atlanta. Cultural differences certainly play a part. Mr. Worthington notes that many of the white teachers who come to his school from white high schools and predominantly white colleges have trouble adjusting to the different speech patterns and classroom characteristics at Avondale. Among other things, he would like to see new teachers learn the true Creole language that many blacks here speak. "I see my kids as bilingual," says Worthington, who received his cross-cultural training as a high school football coach. "There's a language that they use within their own culture that may not be used in the majority culture at large. My teachers should know that, so they can understand what's going on and allow it to be acceptable."

Today, there are signs that colleges are trying to address the exodus as a product of teaching methods rather than latent racism. "[White flight] is a major subject of debate in the literature right now," says Christine Sleeter, an education professor at California State University at Monterey Bay. It is a travesty that individuals graduating from college can earn in their first job offer, more than their professors in most cases. This country does spend billions on incarcerating young black men instead of investing in their education and rehabilitation. Consider these statistics from The U.S. Bureau on Labor Statistics:

On December 31, 2005, there were 2,193,798 people in U.S. prisons and jails. The United States incarcerates a greater share of its population, 737 per 100,000 residents, than any other country on the planet. But when you break down the statistics you see that incarceration is not an equal opportunity punishment.

U.S. incarceration rates by race, June 30, 2006:

- **Whites:** 409 per 100,000
- **Latinos:** 1,038 per 100,000
- **Blacks:** 2,468 per 100,000

Look at just the males by race, and the incarceration rates become even more frightening, June 30, 2006:

- **White males:** 736 per 100,000
- **Latino males:** 1,862 per 100,000
- **Black males:** 4,789 per 100,000

If you look at males aged 25-29 and by race, you can see what is going on even clearer, June 30, 2006:

- **For White males ages 25-29:** 1,685 per 100,000.
- **For Latino males ages 25-29:** 3,912 per 100,000.
- **For Black males ages 25-29:** 11,695 per 100,000. (That's 11.7% of Black men in their late 20s.)

Or you can make some international comparisons: South Africa under Apartheid was internationally condemned as a racist society.

- **South Africa under apartheid (1993), Black males:** 851 per 100,000
- **U.S. under George Bush (2006), Black males:** 4,789 per 100,000

What does it mean that the leader of the "free world" locks up its Black males at a rate 5.8 times higher than the most openly racist country in the world?

U.S. Justice Department reports shows that U.S. prison spending quadrupled in the past two decades, along with the rate of incarceration. According to the reports, the United States spends $40 billion a year on federal, state and local prison construction and operation. For state prisons alone, spending increased from $6.8 billion in 1984 to $30 billion 2007.

Costs of Incarceration and Supervised Release

In fiscal year 2007, it cost $24,922 to keep someone incarcerated in a Federal Bureau of Prisons facility for 12 months, and $22,871 to keep an inmate incarcerated in a community correction center.

For the same 12-month period ending September 30, 2007, it cost $3,621.64 for a federal offender to be supervised by probation officers.

Those figures translate in daily costs of $68.28 for a Bureau of Prisons facility, $62.66 for a community correction center, and $9.92 for supervised release.

For criminal defendants who had not yet been tried, the daily cost of pretrial detention services was $64.40 and the cost of supervision by pretrial services officers was $5.85.

As a black male who has successfully navigated through this sometimes most difficult and disappointing system, here are a few things that we as blacks need to do to ensure the continued survival of the black male:

- Reinvest our money, time, and skills in the community. This applies especially to those fortunate enough to have made it through such a discriminatory system.
- Make sure that our young men are reading and opening their minds to the vast world that awaits them.

- Make sure that we successful black men are the positive role models that we profess to be.
- Make sure that the environment that we as fathers create in the home, is a learning, loving, and respectful one. Remember that being the head of the household is an earned title.
- Take care in how we treat our wives because our boys will become fathers who will emulate what they hear us say and do.
- Keep Christianity in their lives. Don't send them to church, take them to church.
- Teach them how to effectively communicate without slang. The ability to facilitate and communicate is invaluable.
- Teach them to respect themselves as well as others. Step wisely because of the pot holes.
- Open doors for women, it's proper and respectful to those who are the mothers of our nation.
- Teach them self awareness and self discipline.
- Follow the motto that a good *attitude* will help develop your *aptitude* which will propel you to a higher *altitude*.

Why do I mention these facts and figures at this point in the book? Well, it's because I am the product of this same less than perfect system for black men and I am proof that there is always a chance to pick ourselves up, dust ourselves off and stay in the race.

I had finally decided that the military was my key to bridging from a poor socio-economic condition to having the ability to compete for my piece of the economic pie. After all, my brother Bill had gone into the service and seemed to be having a great time. I felt it was time for me to try my wings without the constant surveillance of Mother and Daddy. What propelled me may not be your motivating factor. What is expected though is that you will find out what motivates you.

Chapter IX

Life in the Army

In our daily lives, we must see that it is not happiness that makes us grateful, but the gratefulness that makes us happy.

Unknown Author

Getting into college was not something that I was looking forward to. My grades were adequate in high school but I did not think, nor did I have the confidence that college was for me. After a failed attempt to pass the SAT exam, I was somewhat relieved because what I really wanted to do was follow my brother Bill into Uncle Sam's army.

At the age of 17, I was too young to enlist into the army without my parent's signature. I also knew that it would take the influence of Mama if Daddy was to allow me to sign up for the army. I will never forget the morning at the breakfast table when I broke the news to Dad of my wish to join the army. You could have heard a pin drop. He said, with his signature tongue biting gesture, "Boy, do know what you are saying. You should have yourself off in school somewhere." By this time, I had slid so far down in my chair that you could only see the top of my head. "Boy, sit up straight in that chair and act like you are civilized," he would say. "Go on to the army. You will wind up going over to that Vietnam and get shot up or killed." Those people don't give a rip about black soldiers. What are you fighting for? Who will watch your back? What will you come back to if you come back."

After listening to Dad's tirade on the Army, I realized that I had to go to plan "B" and get Mother to talk to him for me. Mothers had the formula for getting what they wanted from their husbands. My Mother understood my need to develop my independence and agreed to speak with Dad about supporting my going to the Army. Feeling somewhat guilty for going against what Dad had advised, she made a contract with me. The condition of their signing was that I would go on to college after completing the army's three year commitment. It was their wish that I finish college and not necessarily mine. These are the cross road decisions that did determine futures and outcomes. I didn't know what I didn't know.

Things were a bit strained between me and Dad after that encounter at the breakfast table. Boy was he a tough sell on just about anything. Of course, I was confident that with Mama's help, he would soon get over it. It was hard seeing his cold stare for the next few days. Dad was one who held things for a long time. I guess it had something to do with his personal struggles and making ends meet when he would never in his life time be given the chance to be all that he was capable of being. I look back even now at the many lessons that we learned from that old man and they were many. He was indeed ahead of his time.

This was a very difficult time in my life, trying to decide between going to college or going to the army as many young African Americans did after high school. Though I knew the importance of education, I had this yearning for something different. I was so interested in the military especially after hearing the stories from my brother Bill when he was able to come home. He was stationed in Ft. Hood Texas with the 2nd Armored Division. Those stories helped me to make my decision to join him in Uncle Sam's Army in service to my country. Doesn't that sound sweet to say "my country"? Quite honestly, things were not sweet for young blacks during that period. My young eyes were beginning to see what a tough row I had to hoe as I approached adulthood.

I was to venture into a world of uncertainty and racism disguised by politics and love for country. It would prove to be a life of false promises and manipulation of any and everything standing in Uncle Sam's way. It was his way or the highway. Though discrimination had become a continuing part of our world, I was about to learn in a very direct and non-sympathetic manner what being a member of the so called underclass really meant. I was excited about leaving home for the first time but apprehensive about what was out there for me. It was hard seeing mama's tears as her baby left the nest. Daddy showed no emotion at all but I knew deep in my heart that he would miss me too.

The trip to the induction center in Montgomery, Alabama, by way of Greyhound bus is etched deeply in my mind. Some of us were excited and looking forward to a new experience while others were looking for every means possible to fail the test. Guys were eating soap to run their blood pressure up while others were acting like homosexuals to draw attention to themselves in hope of being rejected. Man, in those days, it was really a kiss of death to be identified as a homosexual, especially in a place like the military. By this time it was much too late to change my mind. Don't think it didn't cross my mind after seeing this bunch of weirdoes that I would have to live with as a part of this man's army. It was the first real time to socialize with men from all over Alabama both black and white.

I felt comfortable communicating with anyone no matter their race. As far as I was concerned, they put on their pants one leg at a time just as I did. Even in that induction center, the atmosphere and evidence of segregation was ever so present. The whites sat with the whites and the blacks with the blacks. It was segregation for sure but it was also comfort level. We are homogenous beings and "birds of a feather tend to flock together." Back then, we saw segregation in anything that was strictly white and black. Even though racism was rampant then, those white boys were just as afraid as we were and they were also just doing what made them comfortable. This was to be a lesson in human relations for all of us.

After induction, I was assigned to eight weeks of basic training at Ft. Polk, Louisiana, what would prove to be the character builder for me as far as I was concerned. I was promised by the induction officer that the world would open to me and that I could get a start on my college education while serving my country. The world opened allright and I fell right into it. What he failed to tell me was that the education that I was to get had nothing to do with academics. This was the army's technique of luring many college age men into the armed forces. That was the last time in my entire Army career that I was to hear of any mention of a formal education. Racism was live and well; it was made completely clear as the administrative jobs and any other responsible positions would go to the white troops.

Ft. Polk Louisiana had to be the second set of the worst arm pits in the country. For miles upon miles all you could see was the row houses called barracks, the exercise fields which would take many victims captive, and the miles and miles of dirt roads that we would get to know very intimately through early morning forced marches and physical training runs. My mother had told us about hell but this was the first time that I was to get a personal tour. The wild hogs, snakes, jack rabbits, and armadillos would give us a lesson never to be forgotten. I will never forget the day they picked us up for boot camp. We were loaded onto a cattle trailer along with our newly issued equipment. You are first given $60 which looks very good to kids who had never had much money. Once given a haircut (something shy of bald), the army issue clothing, your boots, and equipment, you were lucky to have more than ten bucks left. We were loaded onto these long cattle trucks with our duffle bags in tow and taken to what was to be our home for the next eight weeks.

As we unloaded the truck, our first nightmare was staring us right in the face. It was called a DI or drill instructor. These were some of the meanest, most discourteous individuals placed on God's earth. From sun up to sun down their voices could be heard barking in the distance like a dog that had lost its master. These voices would make us or break us during basic training. "Move it, move it", would be the command for double time. We were to run any time we left the barracks. It was the DI's job to instruct us in the art of self-defense, survival, and self-discipline in a team atmosphere.

It was obvious that these guys were rejected by their parents, slapped on the wrong end at birth, brushed their teeth with sand paper and was raised by wild dogs. Those Drill Instructors assigned to Eco Company, First Battalion, of which I was a part, must not have been fed for a long, long time, had a bad child hood, abusive parents, a cheating spouse, or needed a change of underwear because they were in a constant state of mean. They could out run, out shoot, out curse, and out fight any one of us. Their bodies were shaped like perfectly carved statues and their tongues were sharp as a double blade knife. I really believe that their mothers named them Sgt. Savage and Sgt. Wilder at birth. Their names were indication enough of what was to come for us.

Most of us were too young to shave but that was not enough excuse to save us from the routine "dry shave exercise" that took place in formation every single morning. After several months of scraping the peach fuzz from our faces, the hair had no problem popping through that once smooth skin. The morning formation or assembly was normally held at first light. The drill instructors seemed to enjoy taking us through the normal paces and ending the morning exercise with a two mile force march in full gear, and prior to breakfast I might add. Most of the white and black troops seemed quite comfortable with each other though the relationship between the officers and black sergeants seemed strained.

The sergeants were more experienced and a lot older than the officers who were their superiors. These officers, in more cases than not, came to us directly out of college or military school and were mostly white. All of the traits that you did not want to see in a leader were ever present with some of these guys. They were arrogant, blatantly racist, and felt themselves much superior to all of us because of their rank. Their "rule by fear" mentality only served to stiffen my resolve to move beyond their style of leadership. They reminded me of the old deacons in the church back home, they did not accomplish in life what they had hoped so they saw the church as a way to satisfy their urge to lead. Just because they came from some of the better schools and had taken ROTC was not a guarantee that they would be good leaders. What they did not understand was that everyone is not cut out to be a leader.

I would not allow them to dictate my life's direction. I would be the master of my fate. I know that many of you know exactly what I am talking about. All of the young recruits both black and whites, were treated as if we were inferior. We were told that we were nothing but lowly grunts that could not make it in the civilian world. Why was I not feeling inferior? Why did I feel that I could accomplish anything that I set my mind to? I kept asking why? Why? Why? To a degree, I felt a slight advantage because I was convinced that I could not only live in my world but I was capable of and could survive in this mixed world also. I really didn't think that they could do the same in my world.

If I was told that I couldn't do something, well you better hold on because you were in for one heck of a ride. I was determined to be the best soldier in the unit and would challenge anyone big or small to deny me. In my second week of training I was selected as platoon runner, an honor given to the most physically prepared and the fastest runner. At graduation, after the first eight weeks, I had a noticeable grin on my face. I was doing this thing my way. I had set goals for myself and had accomplished all of them.

I had defeated both Sgt. Wilder and Savage in the obstacle course, the mile run and had held my own in the pugel stick competition (bayonet training). The hard work and tenacity was beginning to pay off. I spent the next eight weeks at south post in advanced individual training. The activities during this period did not come close to the experiences of basic training. At the end of the eight weeks, several of the top performers during the period were selected by the Pentagon to serve in an elite ceremonial unit called The Old Guard located in Arlington, Virginia. I could see myself in those military ceremonial uniforms. I had dreamed about this on several occasions and now I was to get the opportunity. During the interview process, it was found that I was too short to meet the height requirements. Because of my background, military knowledge, and determination, a special exception was made for me and I was allowed to join this prestigious unit. As the old saying goes, if you can dream it, you can do it. Though we all had to wear shoes with raised soles, my shoes were extraordinarily high to meet those height requirements. It was the mission of the Old Guard to give ceremonial burials to those soldiers who had lost their lives in service to their country. We were also called on to escort the President to and from Air Force One before and after scheduled trips.

The highlight of my career, while in the Guard, was being selected to stand guard at the grave site of the late President John F. Kennedy. There were also low points in the whole guard process. Listen to this: we were required to stand guard around the animal cemetery. These were deceased animals of the officers and their families. It was somewhat demeaning and a waste of time as far as I was concerned. Protect a cemetery from what? These animals were almost given as much attention as those soldiers coming back from combat.

Our days were spent practicing as a part of the firing party or casket detail. All of our movements had to be strategic, crisp and on point. We were taught to be better than the best. We would spend up to six hours a day marching and practicing our gun salute and the burial process. From standing guard to extra curricular activities (It was an environment of competition and challenge). You had to learn to defend yourself because even in those prestigious units there were bullies from all walks. I was always called scrappy because I would not back down when challenged by anyone. I got my butt kicked many a time but they knew that they had been in a scrap. They got to a point where they would leave me alone because no matter the beating, I would keep coming at them until they would just get tired. There was and is no quitting in this old guy.

Things were finally starting to fall into place for the black soldiers in the Guard. The black soldiers held a large portion of the top ranked positions and that was not a fact that didn't go unnoticed. We were being finally recognized for superior contributions to this very prestigious unit. Once a predominantly white organization, the Old Guard was becoming increasingly diverse which didn't seem to sit quite well with the military higher brass. In fact, they were becoming down right uncomfortable with the change. Now I don't understand why a unit once protected from service in war torn areas, was all of a sudden, left unprotected causing many of us to be redirected to serve in the Republic of Vietnam. Never before in the history of the Old Guard had any of its troops been directed to serve in a hostile area or war zone to my knowledge. Not only were we assigned to the war zone but none of us were given jungle training as was the normal requirement for troops sent to war torn areas. This had everything to do with the increasing diversity of the unit.

In August of 1966 Vietnam, though considered a conflict, was beginning to heat up. The rumors had started around the barracks that we were being considered for combat. Most of us just laughed because this prestigious unit was needed here in Washington to continue to serve the President and bury our brave men and women who had lost their lives in the war. After all, who would do it if we were called to war? For weeks after that we heard nothing, but the rumors continued.

On this particular day, we noticed that many of the top brass were meeting at the headquarters building. Normally they would gather anyway prior to a major visit from some governmental dignitary, but none were scheduled to our knowledge. The meetings seemed to go on for an eternity and this simply fueled the rumors. It was the beginning of one war coming in conflict with another. My "war within" was starting to take on an external perspective.

The meetings were held for an entire week and just as quickly as they had started, the many military cars sped away with a sense of urgency. Within two days of those meetings, we were called into our auditorium expecting another parade or show for the big brass. The Major General started by complementing us on our service in the Old Guard and quickly got to the point. "Many of you are aware of what is going on in our country, (long pause) and many of our troops are in need of support in Vietnam. We of the Old Guard are being asked to help the cause by sending troops to support the efforts. Many of you will soon get orders to ship out to Vietnam." You could hear a pen drop in the place. We all looked at each other wondering which of us would have to go. We were soon to find out as lists of those selected were posted in the barracks. Our days of leisure were behind us as some of the Old Guard units were being levied to serve in Vietnam.

What we didn't know was that we would not have the opportunity to get the jungle training that other units were afforded because they needed bodies now. This was highly unusual but orders were orders. In fact, we began to look forward to a little bit of action. What we didn't know was that it would be the majority of the black and Hispanic soldiers who were required to leave Virginia for the shores of Southeast Asia. The Old Guard was once again predominately white. What a coincidence.

The healthy relationship that had molded all of us into a very professional well oiled unit of the Old Guard, would play a major role in our survival in the war. Though life had, in our mind, dealt us an uneven hand, we were determined to make the best of what could prove to be a very dangerous twelve-month tour of duty. To the many black troops who were affected by the first time call up, it seemed strange that so many of us were given orders to serve in Vietnam while many of the less experienced white troops were allowed to remain a part of the old Guard. There was a healthy relationship that had grown between those of us, both black and white, who had been part of the Old Guard. We had learned to put aside our differences and learn to operate as a team. We didn't hold a grudge with the white troops who were allowed to stay in the Guard and not see combat duty. After all, it was not their decision. It was the top brass that decided to relieve the Guard of its diversity.

Though the misfortune of being selected seemed to come our way more than our share should have dictated, we were determined that we would be the victors in the end and we would endure any hardship that the army could throw at us. Actually the lessons learned there on the parade grounds, the cemetery duty, the president escort and even standing guard at the pet cemetery served to strengthen our resolve and prepare us for what was ahead.

Chapter X

The External War

Each second you can be reborn. Each second there can be a new beginning. It's a choice. It is your choice.

Clearwater

It was August 10, 1967, when a skinny legged kid from Birmingham, Ala. stepped off of the military sanctioned 747 into a world that time had forgotten. We were in the Republic of Vietnam. The sky was blood red but mysteriously beautiful. Though the sounds of 50 mm mortars and machine gun fire could be heard in the immediate area, there was still a calm demeanor about this place. It was as if we had been pasted into a different time period where civilization was just a word in the dictionary. This was indeed a land where survival, not color, was the focal point. The situation was much bigger than color, race, or religion, I thought. I was there to represent my country and what could be more apple pie and motherhood than that. The Vietnamese were but a small battle in my war within. Little did I realize that they were fighting the same battle that I and people of color had been fighting most of our lives, the battle just to survive as a people.

Even now, as I fly from one business meeting to another, the sight of that evening and that experience still haunts me today. I remember the blood red sky, the sounds of the 50 mm mortar shells pounding the country-side, the ratta tat tat of the machine guns, and the eye-to-eye stares of the Vietnamese as we invaded their land. Through the noise, there was still a calmness in the air, a feeling of time standing still. Considering this place, thousands of miles from home, a place of death, a land so torn, a kid had died, a man was born.

This was a beautiful land where we were a team, we were Americans, we were one voice. It didn't matter where you were from because you were American. All that mattered was that we were a part of something special, something bigger than race or bigotry or hate. We were there to represent our country, to slow communism, to help the South Vietnamese people from falling to the North and communism so we thought. Why was that spirit of togetherness present in this far off land and not here at home? My war within was becoming even more confusing.

How would I cope? What a heavy load to carry into battle. Shelby Steele, noted author, columnist and documentary film writer, put it this way, "I think one of the heaviest weights that oppression leaves on the shoulders of its former victims is simply the memory of itself." This memory is a weight because it pulls the oppression forward, out of history and into the present in order that the former victim may see the world as much through the memory of the oppression as through the experience in the present. What creates this weight is that the subject will gird itself against a larger and more formidable enemy than the one he is actually encountering. It was the intrusion of the memory of my recent past that had started to influence my present and helped to determine my future. I finally realized that I had just landed in my own private hell, my private war within.

Not only were we ill prepared for the task at hand but whether intentional or unintentional, we were not given the jungle training that was required for others coming to the battle grounds. We were, as they called us, fresh meat straight from the ceremonial fields of the Old Guard. Most of the other troops knew that we wouldn't last long over there and thought us to be paper soldiers. Just as I stepped off the truck from the air field and before I could settle myself into this new world, a voice pierced the air like a hot knife through butter. It was Sgt. Williams of Eco Company Third Battalion. "Get your ass in gear, he spouted. Do you think you are celebrities or something? You think Charlie is afraid of you? Well, let me tell you something, he has a bullet with your name on it. Get your rifle, and vest and get the hell out there to meet him. He has a welcoming committee just waiting for you. If you feel that you can't handle it, then go home to Mama." It was then that I realized that this was to be my home for the next 12 months. His voice reminded me of old Sgt. Wilder and Savage. They must clone these guys because they were all cut from the same cloth, as the saying goes.

It wasn't enough to wonder about just surviving, my thoughts were of how to cope not only with the internal war that boiled within me but the external war that threatened my existence in the God forsaken land. What a tremendous load to have to carry to the battlefield and at such a young age. It was this intrusion of the memory of my recent past that had started to influence my present and aided in determining my future. Not only was I ill prepared for the moment but also we, as a unit, were not prepared for this external war that burned just ahead. We were indeed fresh meat, straight from the ceremonial fields of the Old Guard to the killing fields of Vietnam.

I was now a part of the 25th Mechanized Infantry Division located in Tay Ninh Province, in East Hell Vietnam. As many of the white and black faces looked around at each other, it came to us that each set of eyes could mean life or death. We were forced into a situation where survival was the driving force not color, not race, not religion. Isn't it ironic how in the face of adversity, the color of one's skin seemed insignificant to the occasion. We viewed each other as equals, as team members, as family. Why then and not now? I feel that in Vietnam, we had one common purpose and that was first survival and secondly to defeat the enemy. Love of country and the pride that goes with it goes without saying. In Vietnam, we ate together, cleaned our weapons together, fought side by side, socialized when there was time, and even suffered together when we lost a comrade. Back home not only are we separated by the railroad tracks but by the age old shackles of racial divide. We stay apart because that just the way things are.

Why does it take adversity to bring us together? When ever there is a national disaster where there is loss of life and property, the affected community band together to aid in the survival process. Unfortunately, the disaster was the focal point, not the bonding that took place. Some families never get together until someone dies. We don't value the living and the togetherness, we focus on the dead. This new generation seems more color blind that any other in our history and maybe, just maybe, there is an end to this racial dilemma in sight. Let's hope so.

For the first time in my young life, dying had become a reality. I had to, as stated by author Robert McGarvey in his freelance article *Traveling in the Comfort Zone,* come to grips on my personal boundaries, define and settle in this new world, and decide how to reach beyond that comfort zone in order to survive. As Mama had always told us, "Look to the hills from which cometh our help, our help cometh from the Lord." As I reflected on that verse, a sudden calm came over me and I was at peace with whatever was to come. I decided, at that point, that living was the ultimate goal.

As I lay there in my army issued cot pondering this new world, this new responsibility, all I could think about was Daddy's words," Boy, no one will have your back, you going to go over there and get yourself shot or killed". Well, for good reasons or not, those words became my motivation to live, to prove to him that he was wrong.

Many young men grow up hoping to please their parents, hoping to get that elusive acceptance. I knew that I didn't want to die, especially so far away from my family. As I lay there looking at the ceiling, I started to think about these words and wrote them down:

One bright January Morn,
To the Bagley's a son was born,

He grew through glory a part of them,
In their eyes a priceless gem.

To school he went,
He was never late,
His parents saw him graduate.

He lived his life in Birmingham,
Now he must go with Uncle Sam.

In basic training the worry start,
They had true faith within their heart.

They went to church with faces grim,
They pray, "Good Lord take care of him".

He sends them news of Vietnam,
"I will be alright, don't worry mom."

Aboard a plane he took his stand,
He journeyed to a far off land.

He never thought that he would be,
And important part of the infantry.

With fright and fear in his eyes so worn,
A boy had died, a man was born.

Many will come to take our places,
The joy will leave their happy faces.

Now I have little worry and little fear,
For there is my God, even over here.

Ted Bagley 1966

When I sent this poem home to Mother, she shared it with the pastor at the church and it eventually found its way into the Birmingham News.

Without proper jungle training, the responsibilities that were assigned us were daunting tasks. We were often asked to be point men, "tunnel rats" and "forward observers." A point man's life was usual short because as point, you are required to walk a considerable distance ahead of the main body of troops in case there was an ambush ahead. Unfortunately, by the time the point man realized that it was a trap, he was cut off from the rest of the troop and usually either captured or killed. Normally the enemy would allow the point man to pass through the ambush and attack the main body. I served as point man for several months without incident. I guess that the good Lord was not quite ready for me to go out that way. I also served as a tunnel rat. A tunnel rat's responsibility is to enter the many tunnels and disarm any explosives while looking for escape routes, ammunition and firearms. Again I served in this capacity without incident.

I remember a time when we were on a search and destroy mission in a known Vietcong (Usually North Vietnamese regulars) village. I was walking through each hut looking for their rice storage bends that were usually located in hay lined holes in the ground. As I probed with my bayonet in the soft soil, I let my guard down and did not cover my flank. Just as I turned my back to one of the huts, a Vietcong rush out of the hut with knife in hand headed for my back. As he lunged at me, Sgt. Harold caught him mid air and in one motion, slit his throat. As I said, it was just not my time to die. As the sergeant looked up from his position on the ground, he could see the gratitude on my face. We just nodded to each other and continued on the mission. That was the way of the bush as we called it. We acknowledged each other with sign language and very few words. Sgt. Harold was one of those white boys that didn't see color but saw the enemy attacking one of his own. To this day, I never knew what happened to him. He was transferred out to another unit and we lost contact. Unselfish men like the sergeant are the primary reason that we are such a great nation.

There was still much that I wanted to accomplish rather than dying in this far away land. These comfort zones that are illusions according to Dr. Bobbi Sommers, a San Clemente, Calif., psychotherapist. We calibrate our minds to either succeed or fail because we are afraid to test our assumptions. My assumption was that this was a temporary state that I had gotten into and to get out of the situation, I had to be smart, obedient and careful. I made the assumption also that I was on a team of professionals who would always have my back. Don't think that testing these assumptions are not nerve wracking experiences. Anytime you get outside of the comfort zone, it tests your ability not only to survive but also to excel while doing it.

We were issued an M16 rifle, a flack jacket, four fully loaded clips of ammo, a helmet and a swift kick in the pants, and pointed in the direction of the action. Old "Charlie", as we called them, was waiting for a chance to get at the new fresh meat that had landed. We were thrown head first into one of the worse battles of the conflict in a place called the Iron Triangle. We had no time to think. Rifle shots were whistling by our heads, soldiers were shooting randomly at anything that moved. Charlie, was in our front yard. We were shooting and hoping that our aim found the target. We had fired our weapons in basic training but never at another human being. It's not easy taking a life but when your personal survival is at stake, you do what is necessary. As the smoke cleared, we could see many of the enemy soldiers lying wounded or dead in front of us. The unfortunate part was that behind us were many of our soldiers who had not been as fortunate as we were. We lost five men and numerous were wounded in that battle. There were many more of these rapid fire battles to come.

God had spared me from this initial battle but what was yet to come? How many more of these battles would I have to withstand? Could I survive in this new chapter of my life? This close encounter brought to mind a writing by Shelby Steel entitled *Thinking beyond Race—Who are we afraid of*. She wrote, "We are the seat of all of our energy, creativity, motivation, and power. We are most strongly motivated when we wanted something for ourselves." I wanted something for myself during that battle. I simply wanted to live. Life, at that point, was the most important element, of that bug infested jungle.

I so vividly remember the first time personally coming in contact with a North Vietnamese soldier. We were there to support the South Vietnamese so those from the North were truly our enemy. We were to find out later that there were enemy on both sides. As our battalion was engaging one of the enemy battalions in peak-a-boo fighting in the rice patties in Cu Chi, I encountered a young soldier who couldn't have been more than 17 years old. He was running no more than 30 feet ahead of me and was shooting as he ran. He suddenly turned as if to say, "I am tired and can't run any further so I choose to stand and fight." As he looked into my eyes and my eyes met his, he dropped and screamed something in his native language and started to raise his Russian supplied AK47 rifle to shoot. Scared to death, I instantly took the firing position with my

M16, placed a clip of ammo into the slot and began firing over and over again. All I remember was that I fired until I did not hear any rounds coming from his direction. I had no idea what I was about to experience. Being shot at and shooting at another human being was not an easy task.

As his rounds zinged past my head, for the first time I thought about dying. All I wanted to do was live. My father's words kept ringing in my ears," You are going to go over to Vietnam and get yourself killed." To that point, this whole war thing was just another adventure for me. Reality had finally set in that this was serious and I could get killed. I was finally seeing this as serious business where the struggle between life and death laid in the balance every second, every minute, and every day.

As the smoke from the hot muzzles cleared and the smell of spent rounds of ammo laid smoldering on the wet soil, I raised my head from behind the mound of dirt. I could see a still body laying face up on the edge of the rice patty. I didn't know whether to approach him or stay put. Finally, my curiosity kicked in and I slowly pushed myself up using the butt of my weapon and took a defensive position as I approached the lifeless body of the young soldier. I could hear the battle going on all around me as our troops continued to press the enemy back toward the North.

As I moved closer and closer to this lifeless figure, it was obvious that he was either dead or mortally wounded. A lot was running through my mind. Had I really killed another human being? It brought back the memory of the little red bird that I had killed years earlier. As with the bird, I didn't really want to kill him, I just wanted to scare him enough to see him fly away. I wasn't trying to kill this soldier, just chase him back across the border. That kind of thinking could have gotten me killed.

As I stood over this body, this human being, pictures of his family flashed through my mind. He had a Mother, Father, possibly other sisters and brothers as I did. Just in that brief moment, a life of a person that I had never known had been snuffed out. I thought about him and whether he would be feeling the same way about my family if the shoe was on the other foot and I was lying face down in that muddy field.

As I stared at his lifeless body, I noticed a piece of paper sticking out of his pocket. I reached carefully down to retrieve it and to my surprise it was a picture of his family. Now I was really sick to my stomach. I still have that picture and though I am not proud of this memento of the past, it is a constant reminder of how fragile life really is, how in a blink of an eye my life and the lives of my family could have been changed forever had I been the victim versus the victor.

The days seemed like weeks, the weeks like months and the months like years after that encounter. That was just the beginning of many more similar experiences in that beautiful hell hole of a country. The taking of a human life was not what I had spent much time thinking about. It shows just how naive most of us were of being in such a life threatening situation. At that point the real politics of war had little significance. We were being told that we were there to protect our way of life and to keep communism from spreading to our shores. That explanation reminded me very vividly of the same words that the Klan used to justify their actions back on the streets of Birmingham. I was really feeling like I was intruding in their country. I continued to think of the young soldier that I had encountered. He was also defending his country and we were on his country's soil. I am sure that he had his own personal wars to fight, just as I did. Now we will never know.

As I rejoined my platoon and continued to push our adversaries farther and farther to the north, that one incident had changed me forever. Though similar encounters were to come and many more lives were to be lost on each side, I no longer looked so sympathetically at the enemy. I no longer thought about their families. I now had an attitude of kill or be killed. That had to be the mindset if we were to survive this external war. We were indeed transformed from boys to men. It even surprised me how emotionally cold I had become, how that significant event had turned me from a caring individual to a survivor who just wanted to live. The gangs of our communities today tend to have that same attitude. Something or someone changed them from being caring young people to surviving thugs.

This was a clear example of what Martin Luther King, Jr. meant when he said, "Men fear each other because they don't get to know each other." War results from the inability of governments to understand each other's issues, needs, and cultures. Because of man's need for power, supremacy, and economic superiority, there will always be conflicts somewhere in the world. We would all have our "Short timer calendars" on the wall where we marked off each day that we were closer to going back to the "world" as we would say. The many nights of mortar rounds and small arms fire hitting our barracks were nerve racking. As I drew closer and closer to my date of rotation, my nerves were a wreck. There were many who went through their entire assignments only to lose their lives within a few weeks of leaving for home. I did not want to be a statistic.

The days and nights were slow in coming. It concerned me that some of the white officers and most white soldiers were allowed to come into base camp 30 days prior to their leaving country while the black, Indian and Hispanic troops were normally kept in the field sometimes as late as five days before leaving the country. These things helped to bring to a boil my "war within". What I soon came to realize was that even Uncle Sam's Army was a microcosm of society. There were those who discriminated, those who were unskilled, those who were drug dependent, and those who were power mongrels just like in society.

I made many friends during the war, from all cultures and races. You really develop a bond in war that is hard to maintain in peace. There were many lessons to be learned through war: 1) understand where your rallying points are. Rallying points are places that we would gather if we were ever separated in battle. If there were more rallying points in real life, there would be fewer problems. 2) Take care of your weapon and it will take care of you. Your weapon was your very best friend. It would not let you down if cared for properly. 3) Respect the land and its people without fearing them. After all, we were supposed to be there to liberate them. 4) Groups tend to fare better in tight situations than individuals. And, finally, 5) Trust your instincts.

When the day had come for my leaving that God forsaken place, I was torn between the feeling of leaving friends behind and the feeling of joy for making it to the day where I could see my family again. We would often hear of planes leaving with solders headed home being shot down before leaving the country. Naturally that was on my mind as my day drew closer. You may not believe it, but many of us had second thoughts about leaving our fellow soldiers behind. The bond was much greater than anyone realized. We were not only connected physically because of our duty, we were also connected mentally. We grew to know each others thought patterns which assisted us in our strategic approach to attacking the enemy. As strong as the bond was in that part of the world, it was short lived.

Chapter XI

Home Coming

When the best things are not possible, the best can be made of those that are.

—*Richard Hooker*

When we arrived back in the states at the reception center in San Francisco, we were allowed to go across the river to Oakland for a little relaxation. There were four of us from the same unit, two blacks and two whites. I will never forget that incident. It made me realize that no matter how much has happened and how things seem to change, they still remain the same. The four of us went into a diner where there were only white patrons sitting both at the bar and at tables and booths. We were all in uniform as we made our way to the order counter.

We had been walking for hours and were thirsty and hungry. Our two white friends ordered burgers and drinks and were quickly served. We did notice a sudden quiet that came over the café as we walked in, but we thought nothing of it. As the two of us tried to order, we were told that they did not serve people like us and that we had to leave. Our two white friends, who had been served, walked to a table and took a seat with smiles on their faces. It would have been very easy for us to lose our tempers at that moment but we looked over at our so-called friends who seemed to enjoy what was happening and turned and walked away.

The bond that had been developed in war was torn apart in peace. We were back in the real world, a world of hatred, bigotry, discrimination, and difference. We went back to a world that did not care that we had just risked our lives serving our country, a world that was more focused on the color of our skin and not the content of our character, or the sacrifice that had been made. Why do men of all races have to die in support of a people who view you as "less than"? The war within was boiling once again. As I reflect back on my experience, I choose to see the good physical conditioning, the new friends that were made, the lessons of war, and the maturation, as positive outcomes of the war experience. I truly believe that I made a difference in the lives of those I came in contact with, even those who will not admit it.

When I stepped off the plane in Birmingham, Ala., after returning home, the first person to meet me was my dad, the same person that told me at the breakfast table that I would go to Vietnam and probably get killed. He was finally starting to show emotion, something that none of us thought he had. It was obvious that he was happy to see me. He stood there with his hand on my shoulder, tears streaming down his cheeks. That was the best homecoming gift that I could have received. The first thing my mother reminded me of was my commitment to go to school. For weeks after returning from the war, I had problems adjusting. Everything seemed to irritate me and I didn't want to leave the house. After a few months of adjusting to civilian life, it was time to keep my promise to my mother and return to school. I decided that Birmingham was not the place for me so I decided to go to Columbus, Ohio to live with my brother and his family. Needless to say, that didn't work out because I had the need for my independence.

My brother Bill was working at Lazarus department store as a cobbler and a darn good one at that. One evening after a hard day's work, he came home and asked if I would like to work at the store with him. Knowing that I was to start school within a few months, I didn't know how it would work my having a full time job and going to school. I had enrolled as a business student at Ohio State University. Bill suggested that I work the evening shift and go to school during the day. That seemed a little much but I was willing to try.

School proved to be quite a challenge because I had lost the practice of good study habits and had started to focus less on schoolwork and more on money. Things were difficult for the first year and I barely made passing grades. There were only a few African American students on campus which made things a little uncomfortable. There were no black fraternities or sororities, no black student union, few activities at all related to our culture. After a time, we were able to get a Black student union where we could find comfort, play our music, and study without the stares and hateful attitudes of some of the white students.

After the first year at Oho State, I decided that I needed to go to a smaller college where I could focus, have more teacher contact, and a larger support group. At Ohio State University, some of the key classes were taught by television and any questions were to be dropped in a question box. For those of us who were just getting back into the study habit, it was difficult. It was tough trying to compete in an environment which was completely geared to the white students. There were no support groups in the area for us as black students.

In my fall semester, I made the decision to transfer to Franklin Business Law School where I would have a bit more comfort, smaller classes, more teacher contact, and much more of a support group. In the smaller school, I was able to refocus on what was needed not only to graduate but to seek a career in a very competitive market.

I really enjoyed the smaller school because of the personality and personable nature of the instructors. With school came, more friends, more responsibility, more maturity, more direction. I graduated from Franklin Business Law School with a BS degree in Business Management.

Along with maturation sometimes comes infatuation. I was introduced to a pretty young girl by my friend, Ken Folks, who was a young lawyer in the Columbus, Ohio community that I had settled in. The lady's name was Helen Clemmons. She was the most beautiful girl I had ever met. Ken let me know that she would often walk past my job going to lunch at a little greasy spoon restaurant. We called them greasy spoons because the food was good but the grease would soak through the carry-out bag.

I was very inexperienced with ladies and somewhat shy. The idea of speaking to that pretty girl gave me chills. I was a loader on the truck docks at Lazarus Department Store. She had the most beautiful legs and figure of any woman that I had seen. And to top it all off, girls were wearing mini skirts. Be still my heart. She knew what affect she was having on me so she would make the trip past the docks every day around lunch time. Once I laid eyes on her, there was not enough energy left to do my job. She was gorgeous. I finally got up the nerve to speak to her. It was obvious to the both of us that it was an immediate attraction. We started dating and a long term relationship had its beginning.

It was tough finding gainful employment even with a degree. Helen and I were having an on and off relationship so I decided to leave Columbus for Youngstown where there was a better chance of getting employment. I had made contact with my cousin Herman "Pete" Starks, in Youngstown. He was a city councilman in the 5th district. Pete had all kinds of connections in the area. It was not easy at first trying to get established in a new town. Luckily, I had family in the town and my big aunt, Auntee Evelyn or "HUN" as most folks called her, took me in and allowed me to stay in an attic room that she had. Auntee, was my second mother and I truly loved that lady, God rest her soul. She would plat my hair in corn rows before I went to work because she felt that my afro was too militant looking. My Auntee was from the old school and felt that you didn't want to do anything to upset white folks. She was one of the holy rollers who believed in the tent preachers and evangelists and would give them her last dime to help them do the Lords work. The lady was straight from the country.

Little did she and many others know that many of these holly rollers were nothing but scam artists, praying on the strong religious believers of a people who were looking for hope wherever it could be found. The way our older generation flocked to these tent preachers reminded me of the Jonestown Massacre. Almost three decades ago an unusual series of events led to the deaths of more than 900 people in the middle of a South American jungle. Though dubbed a "massacre," what transpired at Jonestown on November 18, 1978, was to some extent done willingly, making the mass suicide all the more disturbing. When a people blindly follow the teachings of man versus God, another Jonestown can happen. These older Christians in the black and white neighborhoods would give a lot of their worldly goods to these tent evangelists.

No matter how I tried to convince her to go to traditional churches instead of these tent preachers, she continued to give them her hard earned money up until the day the Lord called her home. One thing about Auntee, she believed in something whether right or wrong as it related to her religion and she was as honest as the day is long.

Chapter XII

Entering Corporate America

> *"People are always blaming their circumstances for what they are. I don't believe in circumstances. The people who get on in this world are the people who get up and look for the circumstances they want, and if they can't find them, make them."*
>
> George Bernard Shaw

My cousin Pete was able to get me a job at Youngstown Steel where he worked. Working in the steel mill made me realize the importance of an education. That was hard, wet, dirty work particularly during the cold winters in the northeast. It was particularly difficult because you were on rotating shifts which were not very popular with those of us who wanted to further our education. We had to work in freezing weather rolling the cold, wet steel with only the heat from coal fires to warm us. Many of the men had to work in the rafters above those very hot coal furnaces that actually processed the steel and formed it into pipes. You worked on rotating assignments either rolling the steel to be washed after coming out of the forming furnace or filling the cold barrels used to keep the area warm or cutting the pipe to length to place on the flat bed train cars for shipping. After approximately six months of that life, I had had enough. I did not go to college to settle for a hard labor job in the steel mills. Though I was appreciative of the opportunity, I started the process of circulating my resume to companies in the area.

Within a week, I had interviews both with General Motors and General Electric. General Motors was offering the most money but General Electric was offering a training program. So what did I do? I got on the phone and called my Mama in Birmingham. I could always depend on Mother and Daddy for sound advice in these circumstances. They both advised me to go after the position offering the training because that training foundation would serve me better in the long run and that money would come with experience. My folks were wise beyond their years with no formal education mind you. I took their advice and accepted the opportunity with General Electric in its Warren Ohio Lamp Division. I was on cloud nine because I had finally gotten a real job where I could use my degree.

I was hired as Assistant to The Human Resources Director at the Youngstown Lamp Plant. Though I was happy with my new job, I was somewhat restless and not totally happy with the assistant role. I didn't know why but it just didn't sit well with me. While reading brochures in the office, I ran across a note asking for candidates for the GE Human Resources Training Program in Crotonville, New York. I decided to speak with "Pete" about it. If anyone could get information on this type of training, it was within his powers to do so. What a break! Not only did he know about the training, he knew a person who could assist me in applying for the program. I applied for the program and was accepted. Within a two week period I was off to Milwaukee, Wisconsin, for my first assignment as a campus recruiter.

Prior to the end of my first assignment, Helen and I had mended our relationship and had decided to get married. Though we were on and off in our relationship, we both knew that we were meant to be together. We had a problem though, I still had 6 months left in Milwaukee before moving to another assignment and we could not afford to have her move to Milwaukee for such a short period of time. For that next six months, I commuted every two weeks to see her in Columbus until the assignment was done.

This was another one of those breaks that you only get with the assistance of the good Lord above because only 50 individuals from the better schools all over the country were selected each year for GE's prestigious training program for Human Resources professionals program. Why was this kid from Birmingham, Alabama, given that opportunity? I didn't understand it but I was surely going to make the best it. During my year in Milwaukee, I was fortunate enough to get assignments that only manufacturing trainees were afforded. I got the opportunity because I asked for it. It's the squeaky wheel that gets the grease. After a year in Milwaukee, I was reassigned to the Gas Turbine Business located in Lynn, Massachusetts, as a part of their Union Relations Department. I was the understudy of a guy named Frannie McMantus. Frannie was an old cigar smoking, tobacco chewing Irishman from the local area. Others had told me that Frannie was a man eater and hard to work with. He negotiated the company's contracts with the labor unions. Through this hard exterior, I found Frannie to be one of the kindest, caring and most genuine individual I have ever met. It was obvious that he had not had much experience in dealing with diversity but it was also obvious that he was not going to allow it to come between us. He seemed excited to have this young pup working for him. Many in his position did not want to spend time with the more educated trainees for fear of eventually loosing their jobs. Not Frannie, he had a self confidence well beyond his years of education. He was not insecure at all in his skin or his position. I truly believe that I was the first black to ever set foot in his home. He and his wife treated me like I was their son. I was often invited to dinner. Though the neighbors commented about my being there so frequently, Frannie would tell them to mind their own business. He would take me into the sessions with the International Brotherhood of Electrical Workers (IBEW), THE United Electrical Workers (UE) as well as the Teamsters. I was there in the sessions when they negotiated contracts between the company and the unions. It just goes to prove that an open mind leave room for someone to drop something into it. Frannie was opened minded about our business relationship and it was he who made the relationship a success, not me. He was a man ahead of his time and even in an environment where socializing with the opposite race was not a norm, he valued me as a person and an individual that he had learned to respect and grew to admire.

For those who have not had exposure to the labor movement, Labor unions in the United States are legally recognized as representatives of workers in numerous industries. The most prominent unions are found among public sector employees such as teachers and police. Activity by labor unions in the United States today centers on collective bargaining over wages, benefits, and working conditions for their membership and on representing their members if management attempts to violate contract provisions. The AFL-CIO, one of the unions that I had experience with, is especially concerned with global trade issues. American union membership in the private sector has in recent years fallen under 9 percent—levels not seen since 1932. Workers seem uninterested in joining, and strike activity has almost faded away. The labor force in unionized automobile and steel plants, for example, has fallen dramatically. In another example, Construction Trades now only represent approximately 14 percent of the labor market. The inability to prevent non-union companies from taking significant market share has undercut union membership. It has been difficult for labor unions to retain their membership over the years because companies have taken away their reason for existing. Most labor unions were formed to represent employees who were unfairly treated by their employers in the areas of wages, benefits and working conditions.

Companies today must treat their employees with respect and dignity or run the risk of loosing them to the competition.

American unions remain an important political factor, both through mobilization of their own memberships and through coalitions with like-minded activist organizations around issues such as immigrant rights, trade policy, health care, and living wage campaigns. Unions allege that employer opposition (including running anti-union campaign using union avoidance consultants) contributed to this decline in membership.

Although throughout my career, I had been pro company, I developed a healthy respect for the individuals who represented the union philosophy. They had a job to do just as we did and they did it well. After gaining valuable experience in both Union and Shop Relations, I was sent off to Durham, North Carolina, where the Turbine Business was having some issues with the Ku Klux Klan and The Progressive Labor Party, a communist based organization whose primary purpose, as with the Klan, was to create confusion and dissention among our GE employees. Their interests and ideas were not shared by the majority of the employees at that facility. After our team spent several years playing punch and counter punch with these groups, they decided to move on.

During my stay at the Durham facility, I was under the direction of another manager who was stuck in the mind set that Affirmative Action was another problem to have to deal with. During the early 80's the focus was on Affirmative Action and not diversity. The concept of diversity came about during the turn of the century. Though he hired me, there was no attempt to develop my skills and position me for larger job responsibilities. I have to admit that he did not do a lot of developing of any of his employees. It just seemed that he never spent any time with the minority employees as he did with other cultures. I don't think his racism was blatant, just below the radar and a sign of the times. Though unplanned, I was able to develop many valuable networks while working in that Research Triangle Park where the facility was located.

This was another one of those opportunities that didn't come to people with my level of experience. After several years at the Durham, NC, facility, I was interviewed for a position in Shreveport LA. After returning from the interview, I was questioned extensively by my manager, concerning my desire for another position. He did not speak very highly of the position or of the person that I was interviewing with. It was only later after accepting the position that I realized that he didn't want me to leave. He just didn't know any other way of expressing himself. Actually, he was happy with my performance but had given me no indication of it.

I was hired by the person who was to be one of my mentors for the next few years, Gordon Taylor. Gordon was the manager of Human Resources for the Transformer business in Shreveport, LA. He hired me for the position of Supervisor Plant Relations. After accepting the position in Shreveport, Gordon shared with me the fact that my past manager did not speak very highly of me when asked for his input on my performance. He also shared that it was his honest belief that any one given such a negative rating must have some positives about them so he decided to take a chance on me. He was impressed at how I handled myself in the interview process. A point to remember, no matter how good you are at your profession, you need someone to help you along the way. So be careful how you treat people for you may see them again going or coming and they just may be in a position to affect your future.

From Shreveport, I was offered another opportunity and promotion to a position in Mebane, NC, as Manager of Human Resources for a plant of approximately 600 employees in the Power Systems Division. At Mebane, I received a stern lesson on human interaction. After having a plant manager in Shreveport who was not only a technically sharp individual but one having strong interpersonal and relationship skills, I had the misfortune to work with an individual who was the direct opposite. The man was not technically talented, a very difficult personality, and lousy interpersonal skills. Why me Lord? And the Lord answered, WHY NOT?

This CEO did not, from the very beginning of our work relationship, like me as an individual or professionally. He really was upset after finding out that I was one of his neighbors. Everything I did was wrong in his eyes. It was not until I had had several months of hell on earth with this person that I realized that he had a personal motive for his actions. He had worked at another facility where he had developed a great working and personal relationship with the human resources manager. In order to be able to again work with that individual again, he would have to prove me unworthy. For several months he had marked each document coming from my office with red pens to denote his dissatisfaction with the content. It was his attempt to build a portfolio of errors to be used against me at the appropriate time. What he didn't know was that I was keeping a record of all these documents because I felt that at sometime I would need them.

After several months of our both being unhappy with each other, he decided to call me into his office for a one-on-one meeting. At that meeting he let me know that I was not living up to his expectations (What expectations?) The man had not once sat down with me to tell me what he expected. He let me know that though I had one of the highest performance ratings in the company, he did not agree with it and he would change it to reflect his belief of my performance. I had been rated a code 1, high potential, which he proceeded to change to an average rating. I said to him, "You can change my rating but you can't change how I feel about myself." He was puzzled by my comment and reaction to this obvious harassment. He didn't understand the fact that I had God on my side and with that fact no weapon could be formed against me. A person can only succeed if he or she is allowed too.

Two weeks after the encounter, I was again called to his office for yet another meeting. What I didn't know was that he had asked my boss who was located in Virginia, and the Senior Vice President, who was his boss, to join in the discussion. Once the discussions started, it was obvious that he wanted me out. The group started the dialogue by giving me three options for my career. The first option was to move to Virginia until such time that they could find a suitable position for me. The second option was that I was to remain in the Mebane facility in a lower position. The third option was giving me 60 days to find suitable employment for myself. As they awaited my answer, I just sat there with a smile on my face because I was at peace with the situation. I had anticipated that meeting and had written a letter to Jack Welch, CEO of the General Electric Company, telling him about the situation and asking for an independent investigation of the plant manager. This time, they had underestimated the strength of my network within the company. Jack Welch, had personally gotten to know me after I had made a presentation to him upon graduating from the HR program in Crotonville, New York. Jack not only knew who I was, he had followed my career over the years.

As I sat smiling at them, I opened my portfolio and laid a copy of the letter to Jack Welch on the table. Before I placed the letter in front of them, I made it known that I didn't like any of their options. I went on to state that there was a fourth option and that option was to fire me. They were stunned and obviously taken back by my aggressive attitude. It was expected that I would get emotional and potentially act in a way that would give them the needed ammunition to outright terminate me. They seemed shocked that I didn't react at all. I showed no emotion; I simply got up from the table leaving the letter for the three of them to read. I stated that I would be in my office if any of the three cared to speak to me but as far as I was concerned, the meeting was over. As I started to walk out of the office, the plant manager who had started this mess, asked if I had really sent the letter to Jack Welch. I told him that he would have an answer to that question in a few days. In addition to sending the letter to Jack, I had also copied my friends Steve Dolny and Jim Harmon in Corporate Human Resources.

For the next week, no one said a word to me. Finally, during the second week, a knock came at my office door. It was a corporate auditor sent by Jack Welch's office. The auditor informed me that a full investigation of my allegations was in process. Two weeks later and at the conclusion of the audit, the plant manager was removed from his position, his boss was reassigned to another division, and my boss was forced to retire primarily because he failed to protect me in an obvious discriminatory situation. The audit found no indication of incompetence on my part, many cases of shaky bookkeeping on the part of finance and plant managers, incorrect inventory levels, and many inconsistencies in numbers reported to headquarters. A good example of the old proverb: people who live in glass houses should not throw stones. They underestimated my contacts at the corporate level and they underestimated me. Remember the old saying, be careful of the people that you step on while you are on the way to the top, it is possible that you will see them on your way down. Not only did they underestimate my corporate contacts but they also underestimated the support that I had from the senior management team as well as the employees. You can't lose when you have God on your side. Right will eventually win over wrong the majority of the time.

After a successful four years at that facility, I was promoted once again to a position as Manager of Human Resources for the Aircraft Engine Business in Wilmington, North Carolina. Even at a new location, there was the same war to fight. The one most memorable occurrence at that facility was in the first month of my tenure. The plant manager introduced me as the first Black Human Resources manager in the history of the site. The message that I received was that he saw my race first and then my profession. Had he said, "The first Human Resources Manager who happens to be black," he then would have recognized my profession first and race secondarily. Why did he have to mention my race at all? He wouldn't have introduced a white male in that fashion. Naturally, I could not let that pass.

The war within had started to boil once again. I made it known that I didn't enjoy being called the first black anything because it denoted the lack of progress on the part of the site. If they still had to introduce me in that manner, then there were deep-rooted issues in the facility that needed to be addressed. I have never been one to allow an opportunity like that to go by without giving my unguarded opinion. I have never been afraid of losing my job. Once you have fear of losing a job, fear of failure, fear of speaking your mind in a professional manner, it can paralyze you personally and professionally and will hinder progress. My initial opinion of the site was flawed. It turned out to be one of my better experiences and the senior executive team embraced me with opened arms. There are individuals at that site that I still keep in contact with today.

After four years at that facility, both my parents had started to experience problems with their health. GE, being such an employee oriented company, was able to find a job in Burkville, Alabama in their plastics plant. That decision allowed me to be closer to my family and assist in their caretaking. My Dad had started to experience these mini strokes and for a long time we didn't know that it was happening. What we did know was that his personality was beginning to change. He was always somewhat short tempered but now it was getting worse. My brother and I were going home to visit much too often because of the tension between Mother and Dad. My sister Liz lived in Montgomery and was in driving distance. We all took turns going to check on them.

The symptoms that something was wrong with Dad was that he would hide money from himself. He would take large sums of money and hide it in the garage and in other places and forget where he hid it. When he could not find it, he would accuse mother of taking his money. He remembered that he had the money but couldn't remember where he had placed it. When Bill and I would go into the garage, he would follow us to see if we knew where the money was. Eventually, we had to place him in a domiciliary, a private nursing home. That was tough seeing my Dad in that place. Eventually he got to the place where he didn't recognize us but he never forgot who our Mother was. When we would go to visit him, he would be sitting at the kitchen table writing down numbers. When asked what he was doing, he would say that he was counting his money. Dad passed away shortly after being placed in that facility.

Because of Dad's dominance over her, Mother did not have much freedom to do the things that she loved. She loved to shop, go to visit family, attend family reunions and go to ball games. She did not do much of that because Dad wanted her home. After his passing, Mother finally started to do the things that she loved. Unfortunately, it was short lived. Months after having an operation on her wrist, Mother noticed a dark spot starting to form. Each day the spot would get larger. Not only was the spot getting larger but it had started to flake and itch unbearably. We finally convinced her to go to the doctor. The news from the doctor was not good. Mother had contacted a disease called Scleroderma. Scleroderma is a chronic condition that causes inflammation and thickening of the skin. The cause of scleroderma is not known. Researchers have found some evidence that genes are important factors, but the environment seems to also play a role. This means that inheritance at least play a partial role. It is not unusual to find other autoimmune diseases in families of scleroderma patients. Some evidence for the role genes may play in leading to the development of scleroderma comes from the study of Choctaw Native Americans who are the group with the highest reported prevalence of the disease. The disease is more frequent in females than in males. A common area of involvement of this condition is the skin over the tips of the elbows (the olecranon area). When this skin is involved, it can lead to troublesome irritation of the tips of the elbows with tenderness noted when any pressure is applied.

This is a non forgiving disease that causes it's victims to live in agony of constant itching and dialysis. Mother never gave up hope of defeating this disease and we had confidence that she could. After all, none of us had ever heard of this disease. Seeing how much pain and discomfort Mother was in, we decided to research the disease and see if there was something that could be done to help her. We did find a doctor in Germany who was versed in the treatments of this disease. Unfortunately, the treatment was only good for certain patients and Mother was one who could not benefit from the treatment because her body didn't react to penicillin. The disease finally ran the course of Mother's body on the outside. He skin was hard and dry and we had to constantly scratch her body to give it relief. She couldn't scratch herself because the disease had caused her hands to become hard and brittle and she was unable to move her fingers.

After the disease had covered her entire body, it had started to attack her internal organs, the lungs, the kidneys and finally the heart. Mother lost her fight to this terrible disease approximately two years later.

In my new position as leader of the HR team in one of GE's most automated plastics resin facilities, I still had many personal wars to fight. Burkville was located approximately 18 miles south of Montgomery in Lowndes County, one of the poorest and most economically deprived counties in the United States having the majority of its citizens as blacks and living below the poverty line. GE was attracted to the county because of the tax breaks that were offered in return for agreeing to employ many of the county's residents as well as for the location which was a considerable distance from the heavily populated areas. The products that we manufactured used chemicals that were considered hazardous and had to be transported through areas of least risk to the general population. Rather than take these dangerous chemicals through Montgomery which had the more direct routes, the company chose to take the chemicals through the black townships which enraged many of the city's leaders. Through working with the local legislators, I was able to get the company to reconsider its chemical delivery methods and route the dangerous chemicals through Montgomery which had better preventive methods, better roads and the routes were more direct and in closer proximity to the sources.

Because of the automated nature of the facility, the area schools did not prepare students for the type of jobs offered at the facility. There were jobs such as Chemical Engineering, Quality Control, and Product Development that all required at least a 2 year technical degree. After operating for several years and failing to recruit in the local area as promised, the company began to get the attention of the Southern Christian Leadership Conference under the direction of The Reverend Joseph Lowery. Upon hearing that the SCLC targeting the facility for demonstration, the company's brass decided to get resources in that would have credibility with the county's black leaders. That's where I came in. I had developed, over the years, the ability to negotiate with the community as well as the labor unions in the area.

I was asked to establish ties in the community with the school system and county government. I was commissioned to establish training programs which would allow individuals the opportunity to qualify for work in the facility. The company further developed playgrounds, added temporary housing, repaired roadways, and conducted adult learning classes. During my tenure at the facility, General Electric supported that community to the tune of two million plus dollars, and developed the curriculum in the high schools. Even in a productive society, as was created by the company, there were also issues that fed my war within. One such issue was the job training program designed for those who had been on welfare and those who lacked the skills required to work in our facility. There were twelve people in the program who were given positions in the plant with the hopes that on the job training would be part of the solution. What we failed to realize was that in addition to making a job available, we had to train them on how to maintain and keep a job. All twelve individuals, within six months, had lost their positions primarily because they 1) refused to work overtime, 2) did not want to follow directions, 3) were late coming to work or would leave early 4) took excessive and extended brakes and finally 5) would call in sick often.

It took us a while to understand that most of these individuals came out of a welfare system that didn't require them to get out of bed early, work long hours, or meet schedules. The part that was missing was our understanding that these individuals had to be trained to maintain a job. Though we had honorable and good intentions, we did not understand the social equation that was needed to truly help. After consulting with social workers in the area, we were able to offer these twelve individuals a second opportunity to work at the plant. Only seven of the twelve agreed to give it another try. This second opportunity was accompanied by special training in the art of finding and maintaining a job. To my knowledge, five of the seven individuals are still employed at the facility.

Actually, the company went the extra mile for that community which really made me proud to be an employee. Not only did GE give generously to the training efforts, it also encouraged its employees to help in refurbishing many of the playgrounds in the area. It didn't stop there, the company purchased mobile homes for those in that community who's had long term illnesses and were unable to work and for those elderly who were in need. Now that is a company who put its money where its mouth was.

I had expected that the efforts there in the Burkville plant would lead to larger responsibilities for me. Well, as usual, I was wrong. I later found that opportunities that were available to me were never communicated because they wanted to keep me in the position primarily as the General Electric face to the black community. We had made considerable progress, and to change players, in their minds, was not in the best interest of the community or the company. Because of the rapport that had developed between me and the community, even the community leaders were asking that I remain in the job a while longer, which didn't make it any easier to look from opportunities outside Alabama.

This was a very difficult time in my life because I had just gone through a very troublesome divorce resulting from my move to Alabama. My wife, after agreeing to move to Alabama because of my family's illness, decided that she did not want to move and sent me a note to that affect. That was tough for me because I had given up the position in Greenville, S.C. and had accepted the position in Burkville. One thing led to another and the two of us were in divorce court. After close to three years of court proceedings and close to forty thousand dollars in court cost, the court finally gave us the divorce. This was a low point in my life because I really loved Helen and my family and truly didn't want a divorce and neither did she. Because we both let pride get in our way and also because we both were manipulated, I believe, by our lawyers, we ended as we did.

Not only was my family broken but the court even split the kids. My son decided to live with me while my daughter remained in Greenville, S.C. with her mother. I was truly impressed and grateful that a company the size of GE would make such a remarkable gesture toward one of its many employees. Both parents passed during the late 90s and I miss them terribly.

Prior to my coming to Burkville, the Southern Christian Leadership Conference had called the company to task for failing to hire citizens from the area as agreed upon and as a part of the signed contract to build in the county. On several occasions there were several pickets standing at the entry to the facility just as a reminder of that commitment. It wasn't an attempt to hurt the company but instead to hold the company to the original commitment.

I did enjoy my role in that small community but I knew that I could handle more responsibility and at a higher level of the organization.

After several more failed attempts at a promotion, I finally decided to leave the company after 25 years of dedicated service. To leave after such a long career was a travesty brought on by the "glass ceiling" that many blacks and people of color had to endure as a part of corporate America. The "Glass Ceiling" is that point where you are not allowed to cross. My glass ceiling was executive director.

Not only was the decision tough from the standpoint of having served the company for 25 long and productive years but it was devastating financially also because I was giving up an executive pension over and above the regular pension and based on my executive salary at retirement. After not being allowed to move into the vice president ranks, I decided to look outside the company for the first time at opportunities that were consistent with my skill set. It did not take long before I was offered a vice president's position with the Atlanta based Russell Athletics business. What was it that allowed another company who did not know me well, to offer me a job at that level when the company that I had worked for and succeeded in for the past 25 years could or would not? It doesn't take a rocket scientist to answer that question. Russell was a more diverse thinking company who saw the value in my background and the variety that someone like me could bring to the company and its share holders.

The following years were both rewarding and difficult for me in the new environment. On one hand I grew tremendously because of the international exposure and the restructure of the company. On the other hand, I was somewhat disappointed that I was not as busy as I had been with General Electric. Most of the work in the textile industry was moving overseas and I was like the commercial about the Maytag repairman who had such a good product that there were few if any repairs to be done. I was sitting in my office looking for work and there was little to be found because most of it was in another country. Also, the company, because of its small product margins, was tightening its belt at every end which did not allow for creativity and new idea generation. Receiving a 3 percent base increase after assisting the move of a complete business overseas was not my idea of a reward system. To have moved from a company who gave generous raises of 7-10 percent to one averaging 3 percent did not sit well with me or my wallet.

After spending 2.5 years with Russell, it was time to move on. It was not a creative environment nor were there funds to initiate key initiatives needed to remain competitive in the industry. Next stop was Nashville, Tennessee, as a part of the Dell Computer organization as Director of Human Resources for the Lap Top Division. Taking a job below the vice president's level was a step back, but yet again, I trusted the organization to live up to their word of moving me back to the vice president level after one year on the job and as long as my performance was as expected.

After a year and a half there was still no indication that they were going to live up to the promise so I decided to apply a little pressure to at least get a response. I was one who always spoke my mind and would challenge the administration if their actions were not in the best interest of the people or the business. It was decided that before they would move me to the VP level again, I had to move to headquarters in Austin, Texas, on a lateral assignment. A move of that nature would have required me to remain in the same level for another eighteen month to two years. I was told that my performance in a site location was well beyond their expectations but I still had to prove that I could continue to perform at a high level at corporate headquarters in Austin, Texas.

Why do we have to continually prove ourselves when our white counterparts were not held to the same standards? I saw many other non-minorities who were not as qualified, move past me into levels that they were less qualified based on time in position and experience level. What was very clear in Corporate America, especially the larger companies, there was a pecking order and you had to pay your dues in time, work experience and navigating the political waters to move up in the organization. I felt I had worked hard to satisfy all of the above but opportunities still continued to pass me by.

Though things were trying to change, they were remaining the same. I was not going to allow my career to be manipulated again through false promises so I declined the Austin position. My superiors were shocked that I would pass up an opportunity to work in corporate headquarters. I saw it as another attempt to keep me under the "Glass Ceiling". It was ok to promote us while we were lower in the organization but when we positioned ourselves to compete for the real financial incentive positions, the promotions came to a screeching halt.

There were many attempts on the part of the upper brass to convince me to take the position but I wasn't buying it. They flew me to Austin to meet with several of the senior vice presidents. It was really interesting sitting and listening to senior managers who were more concerned with their desires and the need to have someone fill the position than whether it was the best move for me and my career. I had a choice to make at that point, I could trust them once more and uproot my son and me and move Austin, Texas, or I could take my chances and remain in the current position. I decided to take the latter position and remain in Nashville. I sent a note to that effect to my superior with the caveat that if I was to be continually harassed to take the position in headquarters, I would tender my resignation. In my mind, I could hear them laughing after reading my letter. Who does he think he is? We have him in a good position, a great location. What does he have to complain about?" I am sure they were saying these things. They decided to test my resolve by sending yet another top executive to speak with me. They were soon to find out that money, stocks, position, were not the motivating factor in my decision, it was my self respect and dignity that was at stake, and the fact that I was ready to move to the next level. I wanted to determine my destiny, not to have others do it.

I had my resignation letter on the vice president's desk the next morning. Seeing that I was completely serious about leaving, I had immediate offers to become a vice president and money offers that were completely scary. I was not to be bought so I told them "no thank you." If, all of a sudden, I was valuable enough to be made offers like these, why couldn't it have been done initially and according to the original agreement?

After that encounter they left me alone for a while, but they had stirred up the "war within" once again. I no longer felt welcomed with all that had transpired. If I were to stay with Dell, I would have to deal with a management group who felt that I had over stepped my bounds. It would have affected my appraisals, my compensation, and future opportunity so it was time to move on. A month earlier, I had made a trip to California to visit with an old friend, Brian McNamee. I should have known that something was up when he invited me to bring my skates and roller blades. What a great weekend with an old boss and friend. You see, I had worked for Brian at Dell prior to his leaving a year before joining him in California. Brian and I had also worked on the same team as employees of the General Electric Company many years earlier.

On Sunday, as I was preparing to return to Nashville, Brian mentioned a position that he thought I would be interested in. It was Vice President Human of Resources for the manufacturing sector of the business. This was a surprise and very much unexpected. Up to this point, I had no desire to go to California because of the earthquakes, wild fires, and mud slides. The beautiful weather, the beach, the mountains all quickly won me over completely. Needless to say, I accepted the position where I was commissioned to handle the HR responsibilities for 7000 manufacturing employees. It is now nine years later and I am still in the position as Vice President of Human Resources, Global Manufacturing for Amgen, Inc. Thanks to people like Brian McNamee (Amgen), Gordon Taylor (GE), Steve Dolny (GE), Jim Harmon (GE), Rick Young (GE) and Roy

Perry (Dell), I had the opportunity to realize my full potential in the corporate arena. The significance of this is that all but Roy were white males who were more than interested in seeing this, black professional from Alabama succeed and calm my private war.

The moral of this short book is that anyone can experience their own war within based on individual life drivers and significant events that aid in the shaping of our life perspectives. This private war, this zeal to make a difference has been the backdrop of my life story. This same war was the motivator that gave me the incentive to run faster, try harder, jump higher, and accomplish more toward my life goals. It fed my vision and created a thirst for accomplishment that has yet to be satisfied. It is spirit and drive that I am trying to pass on to young people who are entering the corporate world for the first time. My private war has helped in bridging the gap between the races, by having others see diversity as a means to an end versus another affirmative action program. It is my intention to show how there is a business case for diversity and there is value to inclusion versus exclusion. We can learn a lot from being like the blind person that tends to value the touch, sound and quality of the relationship verses what we see. Our eyes have a tendency to play terrible games on us based on the conditioning process that effects our lives over the stages of development. We often believe what we are told verses what we experience. We go into relationships with preconceived notions that are more often flawed and based on perception not fact.

If you could just experience having a conversation with a group of people in a circle with your eyes closed, I am willing to wager that your opinion of the individuals would be different than it would have been if you had experienced total visual contact throughout the discussion. We human beings form opinions quickly about individuals based on the preconceived information and baggage that we carry into the conversation. When we see things, we immediately start the process of forming opinions and categorizing into our own black boxes.

It's been a blast walking you through the pages of my life. Hope there was something said that causes you to think seriously about your own war within. What makes you tick, what motivates you, what are your hot buttons. As a baby boomer, our final results and contributions to society, have as their roots, our earlier years. *You are what you were when,* as goes the book title. The genesis of this book addresses the fact that your current life holds the key to what was the foundation given in the earlier stages of your development.

Chapter XIII

My Person Beliefs

A man who trims himself to suit everyone will soon whittle himself away.

*—**Charles Schwab***

I truly hope that the journey through these pages has been one that has shows the deep passion for this subject. This was a trip of hope for me and I believe for those of you who can identify with my travels. Some of these experiences may have caused you to remember similar situations in you lives while others was entertaining and most difficult to re-visit and possibly painful.

The pages of this book that you have just completed spanned the period of the 50s, 60s and beyond. These were some of the most interesting, stimulating, yet difficult years of my life. From the racist borders of Birmingham, Alabama, to the shores of Southeast Asia (Vietnam), and on to the rigors of Corporate America is where my "war within" was and is still being fought. The events of this book were as accurate as my memory allowed. I had often wondered how some events in my life have been so easily remembered and ever present while those elusive events are depressed deeply in the subconscious mind. The words on these pages are as I remembered them. I do know that certain of these experiences are clouded by the years on one hand and the pain of recollection on the other.

I believe, as Robert Fulghum stated in his book *All I Really Need to Know I Learned in Kindergarten*, that "imagination is stronger than knowledge, myth is more potent than history, dreams are more powerful than fact, hope always triumphs over experience, laughter is the only cure for grief, and above all, love is much stronger than death can ever be." I do believe that life is what you make of it and not what it makes of you. I believe that life is made up of many Alpha particles and Gamma rays that constantly bombard us with life experiences that aid in our development.

We must view the competition from a lofty position that gives us the ability to look over the crowd, our so called comfort zone. Those of us of color have indeed grown stronger from our ancestry, experience, and just down right determination. We must avoid the dangers of complacency that destroy the strong as well as the weak. We cannot succeed as a human race until we learn to truly appreciate, respect, and value the differences each of us brings to the world's table. Our ancestors gave their lives for our right to be different.

I am at a point that I don't focus as much on Jackie Robinson breaking the color barrier in major league baseball. As important as that event has been for us as a people, I am now more concerned about our young people breaking the "competency barrier". I am concerned that my sons and daughter are given equal opportunities as others having the same or similar competencies. I am concerned that our young men are developing a warped sense of respect for our females including their mothers. I am concerned that schools are categorizing our children as learning disabled without actually knowing who they are or what they are capable of. I am concerned that the country has gotten so competitive and cut throat that people are no longer its most important product. I am concerned that people of difference are automatically seen as flawed and must have special consideration to succeed. I am concerned that the institution of marriage is under attack and broken families are becoming the rule not the exception. I am concerned that too many role models for our young men are their mothers because the men are not stepping to the plate, not finishing school, not attending church in numbers, not holding jobs, and just plain not responsible. I am concerned that the numbers of our young men going to prison is on the rise while those going to college are decreasing. I am concerned that we are allowing TV and video to have more impact on our kids than we as parents have. I am concerned that we, as families, never sit down to a meal together like we once did. I am concerned that reading, writing, and arithmetic are becoming lost arts. I am concerned that, even in the classroom, we are allowing machines to take the place of cognition. I am truly concerned that the things that have made this nation a pillar of strength like family values, integrity, trust, dignity, honesty are being replaced with lies, deception, drugs, divorce, sex and violence. I am truly concerned, ARE YOU?

This short book represents my personal war within. It represents what many people of color have to go through to participate in the American dream or nightmare depending on your point of view. Malcolm X was right when he said that this economic system, this political system, this system as a whole is not geared to a level playing field for African Americans and people of color. For each forward step, the system forces us to take two steps back. It's not good for the affected, those doing the affecting, and definitely not good for America. A nation is only as strong as its weakest point. A nation divided and out of step with itself will not flourish. What is it going to take to make America realize that we as people of color are not going anywhere? This is our home, our country, and we have been a significant part of its past, present, and we will be a part of the future like it or not. The question is, which part?

Our future is rooted in how we are able to coexist one with another. Spirituality and family are the foundation of our culture.

Before you can value me, you have to first see and recognize me. There is a greater power called God that made us all. You may be a little taller, a bit smarter, have more money, look better, work harder, a run faster, cook better, snore louder, and speak more eloquently but this may come as a surprise to you, you are no better than I am with all my faults and I am no better than you. Do you remember earlier when I quoted President Lincoln in his famous Gettysburg address "four score and seven years ago our fathers brought fourth into this continent a new nation, conceived in liberty and dedicated to the proposition that all men are created equal. We are endowed by our creator with certain inalienable rights, that of life liberty and the pursuit of happiness." How soon we forget.

Why can't we stop worrying so much about being Republican or Democrat and concentrate on right and wrong and the values of a nation? Let's stop seeing race and color and focus on content and character. Why can't we see that the enemy is within us and not so much from outside our borders? We are too powerful a nation to be destroyed from external resources, but we can and will fall from within if we don't learn to coexist.

Why do we focus so much on our differences and so little on our similarities? We can't accomplish our aspirations by being a gooney bird that seems to fly backward. They tend to see where they have been before they see where they are going. They are destined to bump into the future rather than lead the flock into it. We, as people of color, are not seeking any more or any less from our country than others. We helped build this nation from an unsure foundation to a world power. We want acceptance, equality and peace for that effort. We never got our forty acres and a mule as promised. I am not sure I even want it if offered because the acres would probably be wasteland or dumping grounds and the mule would have hoof and mouth disease. I am not good at believing promises because I have been disappointed too many times. Believe me I am not giving up or giving in. I just keep giving to a nation that could care less how I feel and how much sweat equity it has taken to continue my private war within.

Am I my brother's keeper? Yes, I am. Take time to see me, know me, touch me, debate with me, share a thought with me, care for me, challenge me, believe in me, compete with me, laugh with me, cry with me. I promise, I won't bite, the color doesn't rub off, I can be trusted, I work hard, I am on time, I do love chicken and watermelon, I cry, I hurt, I make mistakes, but I am just like you because with few exceptions, these describe you too no matter who you are.

My good friend, Steve Dolny, once shared this thought with me: "Have you ever noticed the bumble bee? It's really a freak of nature and shouldn't be able to fly because of its small wings and round chubby body. It does defy gravity with its agility and nimbleness. So why can this seemingly natural disaster of a design called the bumble bee surprise all of us and fly? The bumble bee has long been recognized as vital to the productions of certain seed crops. They pollinate and make possible the beautiful flowers and plants in and around our homes. They are among the few insects that can totally control their body temperature. In cold weather, queens and workers can shiver their flight muscles to warm themselves, allowing them to fly and work at lower temperatures than most other insects. Their large size and heat-conserving hairy coats also help them stay warm."

I know you are asking the significance of this story about the bumble bee. Well, the little bumble bee has a way of adapting. Though they are round with small wings that seem too small and frail to support their bodies, they are important to our ecological system. We, people of color, are like the bumble bee, we have had to adapt to the many challenges that growing up in a world of un-equals have placed before us. We don't always look the part, our dialect is different, our dress is different, how we express ourselves may be different, but like the bee, we play an important role in the balance of nature. We are not second class citizens, just given the title. We are engineers, doctors, lawyers, CEOs, politicians, cousins, aunts, uncles, teachers, policemen and women, business people and unemployed just like the rest of the world. Many of our discoveries and inventions have helped this nation to become the envy of the world. A bumble bee is a bumble bee and no matter how we may want it to change, it will remain a bumble bee. Don't try to mold anyone into something that they are not intended to be. Just let's let each of us become the best we can be and together we will all benefit. What a metaphor.

We are not the same but so what. Each of us brings a diverse richness that that can only make us better. At the end of the day, its matters very little how we start the race or how well we can see the finish line ahead of us. What matters most is how we finish and how humble we remain whether we are winners or losers. I look forward to a day when the need for affirmative action and diversity will not be needed as tools to remind us to view each other as equals. What will it take to get us there? What role can each of us play in bringing this idea to a reality? It's unfortunate that my generation won't experience the joy of this new world. Maybe, just maybe yours will.

The continuing saga as we baby boomers are moving to retirement is who will replace us. This is a dilemma that large and small companies will face between now and 2012 when most of the Boomers will leave a huge gap in the experience and knowledge capital of employers. As these employers scurry to bridge the gap with succession plans and sign on packages, their scurrying may have come too late. Restructures, layoffs, and very attractive severance packages are causing the boomers to leave in record numbers. Those who have invested well, particularly in the securities, are well prepared for retirement.

For African Americans who are waiting in the wings for opportunities made possible by these exits, there will continue to be frustration and disappointments because of their lack of ability to break through the "Glass Ceiling" and penetrate these succession plans.

"Now that is a sermon for another Sunday," as my preacher would say. With the relaxing of Affirmative Action requirements on corporate America, it will make it even more difficult for the underclass to get a piece of the pie.

Homogenous attitudes will continue to feed into hiring and promotional practices. Exclusion by the mainstream of participating in key strategic meetings, sessions on the golf course and nights out with the boys will unfortunately continue to exclude a certain segment of the population. Are there members of the majority race concerned with these matters? Sure there are. Unfortunately their numbers are not significant enough to make a difference in my life time. The unfortunate facts are that those who discriminate are somewhat unconscious of what they are doing. Blacks and women are not given significant responsibility and "stretch assignments" because, the mother hen managers, not leaders, will say "I don't want them to fail on my watch". Actually they feel as though it's their responsibility to save us from ourselves. Whites with similar backgrounds and experience levels are given these stretch assignments with no assumption of failure, so why do they assume that we will fail? I should have the right to fail or succeed, don't you think? These are the attitudes that will, unfortunately, continue to fuel my war within until my time here on earth is finished.

I am very pleased that I have had both black and white mentors in my very successful career. These mentors were very important in showing me both the positive and negative side of survival. Some were legitimately interested in my career and others were going through the motions. Early in my career I was fortunate enough to read the book *The One Minute Manager*, which referred to how truly successful managers operate. Then I followed that reading with the book, *The 59 second employee* which instructed me in the art of staying one second ahead of my one minute manager. The readings taught me to utilize mentors but learn to forge my own path forward. What works for one may not and usually doesn't work for another.

Success is not only about what you know but how well you learn the survival skills, the skills of networking, navigating, strategizing, and negotiation. It's about behavior, attitude and altitude. It's about long hours, learning and mistakes. It's about relationship building, caring and empathy. It's about constructive criticism, developmental discussions and tough love. Its' about you, me, and us. It has to be, it just has to be.

War is made up of many small battles within a greater conflict. It rages on until there are effective negotiations between the combatants. It sometimes consumes the strong as well as the weak. War is defined as a determined struggle toward a specific goal or to struggle or contend. So based on this definition and the content within these pages, I hope that you can see why I chose this topic.

Prior to my completing this book, I was fortunate enough to be a part of voting into office our first black President of the United States of America. What sweet music that is to these weary ears. Barack Obama was sworn into office in January of the year 2009. What does this mean to blacks and the rest of the country? It means that finally our vision should be one that says we can do anything we set our minds too. It gives millions of black youngsters hope for the future. It stops short though of saying that the walls of racism are down. It does take away many excuses that some blacks have centered on our ability to accomplish in this country. It should give us pride that a black man and women will live in the white house and give direction to the country. It also says that we as a people need to clean up our act, place more emphasis on family values and take control of our homes and particularly our children. Young men should see this as a wake up call to pull up their pants first, then their grades and focus on their futures.

Though this is one step ahead for our race as well as the country, this situation must be placed in its proper perspective. Racism is still alive and will be. As long as there are people harboring racial hatred and indifference, we will have separation between the races. As long as there are superior and inferior attitudes, the road ahead will still remain bumpy. As long as there is an attack on the middle class and the "have-nots" are growing faster than the "haves," we will have difficulties. As long as deep rooted stereo types exist between the cultures, we will have more of the same. If we keep doing what we are doing, we will keep getting what we are getting. Maybe Obama can make a difference. Maybe he can help to close the gap between the races. If he is to succeed, he will need your and my help. He can't do it alone. We must continue to place the correct people in both the House of Representatives as well as the Senate. We must participate in the political process and we must move back toward a clear democracy that of "One man, one vote." We must be patient with his leadership because he like none before him, is facing the most difficult task of healing a sick economy, correcting our trillions of dollars in debt, a failing educational system, Wall Street collapse, Alternative energy sources, escalating gas prices and unemployment numbers. Make no mistake, the man has his hands full and can only succeed if the country will pull together and send the message to the rest of the world that we are still the class of the world. We are America the beautiful. Just consider these words:

America The Beautiful

Oh beautiful for spacious skies,
For amber waves of grain,
For purple mountain majesties
Above the fruited plain!
America! America!
God shed his grace on thee
And crown thy good with brotherhood
From sea to shining sea!

O beautiful for pilgrim feet
Whose stern impassioned stress

A thoroughfare of freedom beat
Across the wilderness!
America! America!
God mend thine every flaw,
Confirm thy soul in self-control,
Thy liberty in law!

O beautiful for heroes proved
In liberating strife.
Who more than self their country loved
And mercy more than life!
America! America!
May God thy gold refine
Till all success be nobleness
And every gain divine!

O beautiful for patriot dream
That sees beyond the years
Thine alabaster cities gleam
Undimmed by human tears!
America! America!
God shed his grace on thee
And crown thy good with brotherhood
From sea to shining sea!

O beautiful for halcyon skies,
For amber waves of grain,
For purple mountain majesties
Above the enameled plain!
America! America!
God shed his grace on thee
Till souls wax fair as earth and air
And music-hearted sea!

O beautiful for pilgrims feet,
Whose stem impassioned stress
A thoroughfare for freedom beat
Across the wilderness!
America! America!
God shed his grace on thee
Till paths be wrought through
wilds of thought
By pilgrim foot and knee!

O beautiful for glory-tale
Of liberating strife
When once and twice,
for man's avail
Men lavished precious life!
America! America!
God shed his grace on thee
Till selfish gain no longer stain
The banner of the free!

O beautiful for patriot dream
That sees beyond the years
Thine alabaster cities gleam
Undimmed by human tears!
America! America!
God shed his grace on thee
Till nobler men keep once again
Thy whiter jubilee!

Words by Katharine Lee Bates

As our economy worsen, our jobs go to other more economical countries, our gas prices reach unheard of levels, our 401 K plans loose it's true value, a college degree becomes unreachable for more than half the population, and adds to the destruction of our family values, we must remember that we are still the best there is to offer. We have still the best and most prosperous environment in the world. We remain AMERICA THE BEAUTIFUL.

Chapter XIV

Infectious quotes

As you have seen at the beginning of each chapter, I have used the quotes of many learned individuals from over the years. I have collected many of these and would like to share a few with you that hopefully you too can keep as a collection. These quotes have played an important part of helping to crystallize thoughts and ideas as I have negotiated the murky waters of life. I hope that they can be applicable in your lives as well.

The doctor Martin Luther King, Jr.

"A man who won't die for something is not fit to live".

"You must learn to live together as brothers or perish together as fools".

"Injustice anywhere is a threat to justice everywhere. We are caught in an inescapable network of mutuality, tied in a single garment of destiny."

"We will have to repent in this generation not merely for the hateful words and actions of the bad people but for the appalling silence of the good People."

"The ultimate measure of a man is not where he stands in moments of comfort and convenience, but where he stands at times of challenge and controversy".

"There comes a time when one must take a position that is neither safe nor politic; but one must take it because it's right".

Unknown Authors

"Success can be measured not only in achievements, but in lessons learned, lives touched and moments shared along the way.

"Life ripens at just the right pace. Be careful not to look away, lest you miss its sweetness."

"It is not what you show but what is seen, not what you say, but what is heard, not what you mean, but what is understood."

"To handle yourself, use your head; to handle others use your heart."

"How much you do is important but how well you do it is decisive."

"Correction does much but encouragement does a great deal more."

"The secret of patience is finding something to do in the meantime."

"The more you say, the less people remember."

"What you are is god's gift to you, but what you make of yourself is your gift to God."

"An open mind leaves a chance for someone to drop a worthwhile thought into it."

"Life is an eternal struggle to keep one's earning capacity up to ones yearning capacity."

Experience is like money; just when you think you have enough of it, something happens to make you wish you had more.

"Everyone can give pleasure in some way; one person may do it by coming into a room and another by leaving."

"Finding fault with someone else's program is no substitute for one of your own."

The past can not be changed but the future is still in your power.

Known Authors

Irving Kristol

"A friendship founded on business is better than a business founded on Friendship."
John D. Rockefeller

"If anything can go wrong, it will and usually at the worse possible time."
Murphy's Law

"One cannot be envious and happy at the same time."

Henry Greber

"Ethics, equity and the principals of justice do not change with the calendar."

David Lawrence

"True greatness has little if anything to do with true rank or power."

John Lubbock

"Initiative is doing the right thing without being told."

Victor Hugo

"You will become as small as your controlling desires, as great as your dominant aspirations."

James Allen

"Indecision has crumbled the foundation of numberless air castles and stamped out the happiness of millions of homes."

Dr. Paul Parker

"The difference between intelligence and education is this . . . . intelligence will make you a good living."

Charles F. Kittering

"Enthusiasm is the mother of effort, and without it nothing great was ever accomplished."

Ralph Waldo Emerson

"The declaration of Independence is a kind of war song; a stately and passionate chant of human freedom."

Moses Coit Tyler

"We are born with two eyes and one tongue in order that they may see twice as much as they say."

Romanian Proverb.

"Where the heart is willing it will find a thousand ways, but where it is unwilling it will find a thousand excuses."

Dayak Proverb (Borneo)

"Seek not proud riches, but such as thou mayest get justly, use soberly, distribute cheerfully, and leave contentedly."

Francis Bacon

"The greatest way to live with honor in this world is to be what we pretend to be."

Socrates

"Great minds discuss ideas, average minds discuss events, small minds discuss people."

Eleanor Roosevelt

"The sunshine that lifts the clouds from our lives is the love that we have for others"

Douglas M. Lawson

"What I must do, is all that concerns me, not what people think."

Ralph Waldo Emerson

"Everything starts as somebody's daydream."

Larry Niven

"Love will never reject others. It is the first to encourage and the last to condemn."

Barb Upham

"Circumstances are the rulers of the weak; they are but the instruments of the wise."

Samuel Loven

The opportunity to practice brotherhood presents itself every time you meet a human being.

Jane Wyman

All material things in life are meaningless if a man hasn't discovered what's underneath them."

Thomas L. Phillips

See that no day passes, in which you do not make yourself a somewhat better creature.

John Ruskin

People mistakenly assume that their thinking is done by their head; it is actually done by the heart which first dictates the conclusion, then commands the head to provide the reasoning that will defend it.

Anthony De Mello

Some individuals dream of great accomplishments, while others stay awake and do them.

Beth Lukens

Always do more than what is required of you.

George S. Patton

Hold a true friend with both hands.

African Proverb

We cannot help men permanently by doing for them what they could and should do for themselves.

Abraham Lincoln

It is better to dare mighty things, to win glorious triumphs, even though checked by failure, than to take rank with those poor spirits who neither enjoy much nor suffer much, because they know not victory nor defeat.

Theodore Roosevelt

We find comfort among those who agree with us and growth among those who don't.

Frank A. Clark

If you are going to achieve excellence in big things, you develop the habit in little matters. Excellence is not an exception; it is a prevailing attitude.

Colin Powell

Learn to get along with people, exhibit patience, respect other men's ideas and opinions, think problems through, put yourself in the other fellow's place, be democratic, be loyal, cultivate cheerfulness, and work.

Harry J. Klinger

Alone we can do little; together we can do so much.

Helen Keller

People think responsibility is hard to bear, but it's not. You have a great feeling of importance. I think sometimes it is the absence of responsibility that is harder to bear.

Henry Kissinger

Judge each day not by the harvest you reap, but by the seeds you plant.

William Arthur Ward

All evidence is that luck is to a large extent self-generated. If you want to change your luck, change your attitude.

John E. Gibson

When we cannot bear to be alone, it means we do not properly value the only companion we will have from birth to death—ourselves.

Eda LeShan

It is better to deserve without receiving, than to receive without deserving.

Robert G. Ingersoll

Impossible is a word found only in the dictionary of fools.

Napoleon Bonaparte

Lack of willpower has caused more failure than lack of intelligence or ability.

Flower A. Newhouse

You do not determine your success by comparing yourself to others, rather by comparing your accomplishments to your capabilities. Do the best you can with what you have.

Zig Ziglar

Treat the earth well. It was not given to you by your parents. It is loaned to you by your children.

Kenyan Proverb

A decision is made with the brain. A commitment is made with the heart. Therefore, a commitment is much deeper and more binding than a decision.

Nido Qubein

Be gentle with yourself, learn to love yourself, to forgive yourself, for only as w have the right attitude toward ourselves can we have the right attitude toward others.

Wilfred Peterson

Words of comfort, skillfully administered, are the oldest therapy known to man.

Louis Nizer

Peace cannot be kept by force. It can only be achieved through understanding.

Albert Einstein

To speak gratitude is courteous and
Pleasant, to enact gratitude is generous and noble, but to live gratitude is to touch heaven.

Johannes A. Gaertner

He who looses wealth loses much; he who loses even one friend loses more; but he that loses his courage loses all.

Miguel de Cervantes

Stretch yourself—unused talent seldom grow.

Unknown

Each Generation is a tenant on this planet who will leave a legacy for their heirs. If we guard natural resources, physical affluence and affluence of the spirit go hand in hand.

Stewart Udall

Conclusion

"LIFE ISN'T ABOUT WAITING FOR THE STORM TO PASS . . . its learning how to dance in the rain"
Author Unknown

Our ability as a nation to become one nation under God indivisible with liberty and justice for all is rooted in our not just tolerating each other but legitimately embracing each other as a part of the human family and adjusting our attitude toward one of acceptance and respect for one another. That's right! I said family, that intact group of people having similar wants and needs.

Charles Swindoll, evangelical Christian pastor, educator and radio preacher, said that the longer he lives, the more he realize the impact of attitude on life. He said that attitude to him is more important than fact. It is more important than the past, than education, than money, than circumstance, than failures, than success than what other people say or do. It is more important than appearance, giftedness or skill. It will make or break a company, a church a home. He goes on to say that the remarkable thing is that we have a choice every day regarding the attitude we will embrace for that day. We cannot change our past. We can't even change the fact that people will act in a certain way. We can not change the inevitable. The only thing that we can do is play on the one string that we have, and that is attitude. He is convinced that life is 10 percent what happens to you

and 90 percent of how we react. So it is with all of us, we are indeed in charge of our attitudes.

What are we afraid of? As noted in author Shelby Steel's article, *Thinking beyond Race*, she wrote that we are the seat of all of our energy, creativity, motivation and power.

We are most strongly motivated when we want something for ourselves. Why can't we want to be a family of people with varied, wants, needs, backgrounds and even a few flaws? Ralph Ellison from one of his novels, *The Invisible Man*, wrote that the black problem is not actually one of creating the uncreated conscious of our race, but of creating the uncreated features of our face. That sounds confusing but what he is saying is our tasks are that of making ourselves individuals. We create the race by creating ourselves and then, to out great astonishment, we will have created something far more important. We will have created a culture.

In all our infinite wisdom, our true capabilities are as embryos' laying dormant in the womb of our fears. The umbilical cord exposed to the potential damage which could cut off our food supply. What makes us vulnerable is our own inhibition to love one another as God has loved us all.

On a final note . . . . No matter how much we point the finger at the school system for failing our kids, the thumb always points back at the real culprits . . . . us. A few questions come to mind: 1) Are there rules and guidelines around study habits in the home? 2) Do your kids have responsibilities around the house? 3) Do you do a check of their rooms from time to time? 4) Do you really listen to your kids? 5) Do you monitor TV time? 6) Do you sit together and communicate over dinner? 7) Is there bonding time for both boys and girls with the parent?

Now parents, there could be reasons for our inattentiveness but it's time for us to reestablish ourselves as leaders of our families and stop relinquishing that duty to our children for the purpose of keeping them happy. If you are questioning whether you should

take more of a leadership role, just consider this: Who pays the bills? Who pays the taxes? Who puts food on the table? Who handles family business? Who pays for school, etc.? If the answer to this question is a resounding, "My kids", then my case is a weak one? I have a sneaking suspicion that the parents will come out on top in this debate.

Many in the black communities were upset when Bill Cosby challenged us to not place the blame on others but focus our attention on us. He challenged us to take control over our own destiny and demand stronger efforts on the parts of our kids. Bill was correct; we can and must do better if our young men and women are to compete domestically and globally in a progressively competitive market place. We can learn a lot from out parents and grandparents who, in many cases, grew their own meat and vegetables. They got up early in the morning to tend their crops, feed the animals and bring water from the well because they knew that by being dedicated and diligent to their cause, they would be guaranteed the basic life requirements. Also, they were sticklers about the cleanliness of the home and grounds around it. I remember those two weeks that my brother and sister and many of our cousins were shipped off to our Grandparents home to spend 2 weeks during the summer.

Though we had a lot of fun during those two weeks, my grandparents made sure that we knew the meaning of work. I will never forget the old straw broom that grandmother used to sweep the front and back yards. Yes I said, sweep the yard. In the country, the yard was dirt not grass and it was to be kept clean. The way that she knew that we had completed the job correctly was that the old straw broom left scratch marks in the dirt. She would look for the scratch marks and if there were areas where there were no scratches, you had to do it over again until you got it right. Those old folks paid a lot of attention to details. The one think about farm life was that people were poor and didn't know it because they had

food, their land and a few clothes to keep the elements in check. Above all, they were happy.

These are life lessons that we all can identify with. Let's not let our lives get so full of the day to day living that we forget to live. That we don't take the time to listen to our children, that we fail to give them the nurturing and attention that they need for their development. Sometimes we are so busy flying from place to place to make ends meet, that we become disconnected with those closest to us. When we break the circuit, the light goes out. Reconnect that same circuit, the light returns. As it is with our lives, the relationships that we develop are our circuits and the broken relationships are the circuit breakers. As long as there is a complete circuit, we are in the light. As soon as the breaker is tripped, we are immediately thrust into darkness. At this point, we depend completely on our touching a nearby object to study or position.

The Journal of Blacks in Higher Education states that nationally, the black student college graduation rate remains a dismally low 43 percent. But the college completion rate has improved by four percentage points over the past three years (2005-2009). As ever, the black-white gap in college graduation rates remains very large and little to no progress has been achieved in bridging the divide. William J. Edwards, Assistant Professor of Biology at Niagara University, stated that, "Education is the source of all we have and the spring of all our future joys".

Christianity has played a major role in my life. I was forever in church for choir rehearsals, bible study, prayer meetings, etc. These initiatives were a tremendous help in establishing self esteem, character, confidence and belief in a higher power. Religion has been the back bone of existence for many of us no matter the race or culture. It gives us a true beginning as well as helps us to determine what is considered right and wrong. It tends to cause us to take the right fork in the road, do the right thing, have a clear conscious, keep our family together, adds stability to our daily lives. Now, that's

how I see it affecting me. How does it affect you? We face a society that can be cajoling and menacing and Religion, Christianity, and fellowship has a calming effect on these worldly conditions.

Thanks for taking the journey with me. I am eternally grateful that you have allowed me to invade your world. We are here but a moment so p-l-e-a-s-e make your moment count.

Recommended Reading

Robert Fulghum: All I really Need to Know I Learned In Kindergarden-Uncommon Thoughts on Common Things. Ivy Books: New York 1986

Dr. Wayne W. Dyer: Manifest Your Destiny—The nine spiritual principals for getting everything you want. Harper Collins: New York 1997.

Bill Guillory, Phil Davis: How To Become A Total Failure—The Ten Rules of Highly Successful People. Innovations International, Inc. :Utah 2008.

The National Urban League: The State Of Black America. New York 1993.

Douglas Brinkley: Rosa Parks—A Life. Penguin Group. New York 2000.

www.ingramcontent.com/pod-product-compliance
Lightning Source LLC
Chambersburg PA
CBHW021105080526
44587CB00010B/388